THE PRESIDENT
AND PUBLIC OPINION

Leadership in Foreign Affairs

By Manfred Landecker

Public Affairs Press, Washington, D. C.

About the Author

Manfred Landecker received his B.A. from Syracuse University and his M.A. and Ph.D. at the School of Advanced International Studies of the Johns Hopkins University. After serving in the armed forces for two years, he was associated with the Bologna Center of the School of Advanced International Studies in Italy for three years. He has been teaching in the Government Department of Southern Illinois University since 1959.

Copyright, 1968, by Public Affairs Press
419 New Jersey Avenue, S. E., Washington, D. C. 20003

Printed in the United States of America
Library of Congress Catalog Card No. 68-31163

PREFACE

At present our country is again confronted by a difficult crisis overseas. Many citizens are deeply disturbed by and disenchanted with
American foreign policy. Both citizens and political leaders are once
more faced with perplexing and challenging issues similar to the
questions raised in this study. Journalists have often noted President
Johnson's almost obsessive interest in public opinion polls. The comparison he reportedly made between the Vietnam situation and the
gap which separated the isolationists from the interventionists before World War II indicates a strong awareness of the lessons of the
past.

A careful examination of the effect of public opinion on past presidential decisions can be of value in several respects. History does not
repeat itself, but an evaluation of previous circumstances which
aroused special public interest can sharpen our analytical faculties
and enhance our understanding of the role and influence of public
sentiment in the present crisis. There are certainly some lessons
which we can extract from past experience – although we must be
wary of applying these lessons automatically under quite different
conditions.

Although with respect to foreign policy the chief executive wields
far more power today than ever before, the determination of the
best course to follow is only half the challenge confronting him.
Dramatic changes in communications and education have greatly
enlarged the size of the potential public seriously concerned about
international affairs. The winning of public confidence and understanding, if not support, is the other part of the challenge which must
be met, particularly when the nation pursues a complex and dangerous goal.

We know the President is attentive to the public voice, yet the
record indicates that, like others before him, he may be inclined to
follow his own counsel. The vital question remains: to what extent
does the President lead and to what extent does he follow public
opinion? Considerable evidence indicates that President Johnson
appreciates the nature of this persistent dilemma.

We know considerably less about the effect of public opinion on
presidential leadership than we know about the effect of leadership

on public opinion. Although accurate research techniques have been developed to measure various aspects of mass opinion, we can only hazard a judgment as to what extent the chief executive has been influenced by public opinion.

The present work does not limit itself to a narrow definition of public opinion. Anyone familiar with the profusion of words on this subject will sympathize with the comment by V. O. Key, Jr. that "for purposes of political analysis one need not strain painfully toward the formation of a theoretical representation of an eerie entity called 'public opinion.'" Francis G. Wilson observes that there are "almost as many definitions as there are experts on the subject." For our purposes Key's definition that public opinion "may simply be taken to mean those opinions held by private persons which governments find it prudent to heed" is particularly applicable.

An analysis of the chief executive's reaction to public sentiment cannot, of course, ignore the role he plays in shaping the very pressures which bear upon him. It is his responsibility to utilize all the means at hand to educate the public, so that the wishes of the citizenry will eventually coincide with the wishes of the leadership. Only in this way can an executive decision truly become a national policy.

We can trace the various pressures on the President; but in the final analysis it is very difficult to evaluate the manifold influences which play a part in the decision-making process. President Kennedy observed that the presidency "is mysterious because the essence of ultimate decision remains impenetrable to the observer — often, indeed, to the decider himself." Theodore C. Sorensen has pointed out that President Kennedy referred to the "multiplicity of factors" that are involved in decision, and he reminds us that President Truman once stated that "no one can know all the processes and stages [of a President's] thinking in making important decisions."

There are several valuable studies about the role of the polls, pressure groups, and the Congress, particularly with regard to their influence on the formulation of foreign policy during the years dealt with in this study. For this reason we emphasize those aspects of opinion (e.g., opinion elite) which have received relatively meager attention. However, since all the various public pressures must be borne in mind, an effort is made in these pages to identify and assess how they influence the President's decisions.

In the first chapter we evaluate the theoretical aspects of public opinion in a democracy, with special reference to foreign affairs. In subsequent chapters we examine selectively some aspects of public opinion as it affected Presidential leadership and administration policy during two periods of international crisis. The first period we study covers the years immediately prior to the outbreak of World War II; primary emphasis is placed on the years 1939-1941; the second period encompasses the years after World War II, from 1945 to 1949.

I believe sufficient evidence is available in our first case study to demonstrate that President Roosevelt recognized the important role of public opinion and weighed this influence carefully in many of his political and foreign policy decisions. However, he was caught in a vise between those who urged him to act more vigorously on behalf of the allies and those who insisted on the maintenance of a policy of isolation.

The influence of the public on President Truman's decisions is more difficult to evaluate. There is a considerable element of hindsight involved in his own assessment of the role public opinion played in his decisions, but it is apparent that he had a clear-cut vision of his executive responsibilities and an appreciation of the educative functions of the executive office, particularly in regard to foreign affairs.

It is my hope that this book will make a useful contribution to the efforts of other scholars and practitioners of government to discover how a democratic society in the nuclear age can best employ an effective executive leadership which remains responsive to the ephemeral yet powerful force we call public opinion. We must solve this problem, so that our national weath, talents, and strength can best be utilized in the building of a more secure and peaceful world.

I am grateful to my family for its devoted patience and confidence that this study would one day be completed. My colleagues at Southern Illinois University were a constant source of encouragement. An extensive debt is also owed to professors at Syracuse University and the School of Advanced International Studies of the Johns Hopkins University for their inspiration. Many librarians gave generously of their time, knowledge, and experience and led the way to elusive documents. I look back with pleasure on my visits to the Roosevelt and Truman Libraries and recommend them to the harassed scholar for concentrated contemplation and study.

MANFRED LANDECKER

Department of Government
Southern Illinois University

CONTENTS

PART ONE: INTRODUCTION

I   Leadership and Public Opinion   1

PART TWO: THE ROOSEVELT PATTERN

II   The Shadow of a Crisis   11

III   After Munich   21

IV   The Shadow Lengthens   30

V   Cabinet Members in the Breach   37

VI   A Sampling of Elite Opinion   49

VII   Poised at the Brink   57

PART THREE: TRUMAN'S APPROACH

VIII   The President Explains His Role   63

IX   The Public View of the Soviet Union   69

X   Demobilization   73

XI   Focus on Crisis Tensions   77

XII   The Citizenry Alerted   81

XIII   The Marshall Plan and Korea   92

PART FOUR: CONCLUSION

XIV   Contrasts and Comparisons   102

References   114

Index   132

"The basis of our government being the opinion of the people, the very first object should be to keep that right."

—*Thomas Jefferson*

Chapter I

LEADERSHIP AND PUBLIC OPINION

Before we examine some of the special characteristics necessary for an understanding of the foreign policy-making process, we must ascertain the relationship between government and public opinion. We must determine how government communicates and with whom it is communicating. How does government determine the level of public interest and understanding? How do free elections serve as constraints on leadership? How effective are these constraints? What is the relationship between rationality and irrationality? How can one distinguish between democratic practice and democratic theory? And, finally, what is the role of the citizenry in determining foreign policy, and to what extent should the President promote consensus for a given policy? Each generation must give these questions serious consideration in accordance with the requirements and traditions of its political system.

In foreign policy-making, the conditions of public participation and the span of public influence are constantly changing. Although one cannot determine the extent to which the relationship between public opinion and leadership in this area is more pertinent today than before, it is certain that in this generation, characterized as it is by "crisis diplomacy," the influence of public sentiment must be kept in the foreground in any analysis of foreign affairs. We must bear in mind that the contemporary ideological conflict and the advent of the atomic age have modified the conditions under which public opinion can effectively operate within a democratically organized form of government.

To comprehend the relationship between public opinion and foreign policy one must first understand the basic relationship between citizens and their government. Any organization that is called upon to make vital decisions, sometimes under urgent pressures, requires a decision-making process involving a chain of command. The only alternative for a state would be chaos or anarchy. Since no group of citizens is able or even willing to make the specific choices that confront the state in its regular contacts with other states, we must give up some individual freedom in order to reinforce certain of the broader freedoms which apply to the whole community. This submission to leadership does not imply the sacrifice of the right to make value-judgments or moral choices on issues of public policy.[1]

The leaders of a democratic government, as Hans J. Morgenthau has reminded us, are responsible to the people and are aware that they can maintain their office only by popular approval reiterated at prescribed intervals. If the government does not ascertain the preferences of the citizenry or goes contrary to these preferences, the people may withdraw their support at the polls. Yet while public opinion is a source of democratic legitimacy, it cannot, of course, be the ultimate arbiter of every governmental decision. Morgenthau has emphasized that governments should derive their consent to action from elections, not from public opinion polls.[2]

What, then, is the nature of the "consent" achieved through the election process? Manifestly, presidential elections provide a significant indication of the public mood.[3] Robert A. Dahl, in analyzing the link between elections and policy choices, states: "In an area as critical as foreign policy, the evidence is conclusive that year in and year out the overwhelming proportion of American citizens makes its preferences effective, if at all, by no means other than going to the polls and casting a ballot."[4] If this were not the case, the electoral process would be a very unsatisfactory means of indicating policy preferences.

Unfortunately, foreign policy issues are seldom discussed with calm and clarity during presidential elections. Dexter Perkins, while admitting that an election may highlight a public mood, notes that the hit-and-run tactics of partisan politics during political campaigns do not lend themselves to profitable post-election evaluations of what precisely "it is that has been decided," nor do they serve "to separate one problem from another or to measure with any degree of accuracy exactly what the public response was on the given foreign policy question at issue."[5] Historical experience indicates several problems. "It has been difficult," Perkins states, "to give to a single question in the field of foreign policy a central position in a Presidential campaign; that the natural tendency of candidates for office is to blur, rather than to define sharply, the specific issue; that there is an understandable disposition to retrospective judgment rather than to clearcut affirmation with regard to the future; that it is easy to resort to shibboleths and abstractions in a way that does little to clarify urgent issues of policy; that the point of view of large groups of voters, particularly the ethnic groups, hampers candid discussion; and that in the heat of the partisan struggle positions may be taken from which it is difficult to retreat."[6]

More recently a number of scholars have raised challenging questions about the legitimacy of the election process as an indicator of the will of the majority. The evidence presented in *The American Voter*[7] emphasizes the difficulty of determining preferences on the basis of elections because the voters' lack of information and interest shows that "policies and issues play a small part in most voters' decisions; that only a small fraction of the electorate display anything that could reasonably be called an ideology or organized structure of values; and that voters frequently do not know which party stands for what."[8] Accordingly one political scientist has expressed the view that the absence of a relationship between voting and policy formation may in the future "throw doubt on the efficacy of voting as a democratic control."[9] Professor Key, expressing similar scepticism, observes that "the more I study elections the more disposed I am to believe that they have within themselves more than a trace of lottery."[10]

If the electoral process does not serve as an effective check on the executive, we must conclude that the most valid constraints retained by the people in a democracy are dependent upon the free exchange of information, the right to debate, and the freedom to criticize administration policy. Given adequate implementation, these rights assure that in the long run a foreign policy will be responsibly formulated and developed and that an administration will be held fully accountable for its actions.

Ironically, one of the most significant and crippling constraints that could be placed on public opinion is not a result of strong leadership, but is rather the result of lack of leadership. There is a substantial correlation between the effectiveness demonstrated by the government in the formulation and execution of policy and the capacity of the public to evaluate alternatives or to reject policy. Nothing could be more detrimental to the democratic process than the inability to focus discussion because of inadequate leadership. At best, under these circumstances, "public discussion is left with little other function than attack or criticism."[11]

When the executive branch determines a course of action, it utilizes the generally recognized channels of communication such as the newspapers and the broadcasting media to win public approval for its policy. Whether or not the leadership seeks public support before or after a course of action has been decided upon, the purpose of the approach to the public is to gain approval, to provide a favorable climate of opinion for the execution of governmental policy. Generally there is fairly wide discussion, debate, and criticism, particularly among various foreign policy elites.[12] The views expressed by these elites are important because of their influence on the "attentive public."[13]

By means of education and guidance a citizen may assimilate the torrents of loosely organized facts so often presented in an emotional context. In so far as the information for the attentive and general public is concerned, its presentation on television, in the popular magazines and the daily newspaper is at best analytical and accurately descriptive; at worst, it is sensational and prejudiced. The average individual is poorly equipped by training or inclination to evaluate facts, which often support reactions ranging from confusion, hatred, and fear to apathy. Only in the most broad sense can we speak of a climate of opinion among the general public, favoring perhaps the use or restraint of American power, or the promotion of a negotiated peace based on compromise.

Governmental attempts to win the support of what Almond calls the opinion elite are more complex in that official policy is exhaustively examined by this group. The attentive public is usually attuned to policy review and strongly influenced by its outcome. If considerable dissatisfaction with a strategy develops, there may well be a modification in its application. On the other hand, what will occasionally trouble the opinion elite may have no practical relationship to the successful application of a policy. Such instances call for reassuring guarantees which will help to win support or understanding for a particular plan, such as President Truman's assurance that his request for a four hundred million dollar appropriation for Greece and Turkey would not undermine the United Nations.

Although the submission of foreign policy issues to the public usually has nothing to do with the successful pursuit of a policy in the short run, public review is essential to the meaningful operation of our system of government. It is not surprising that the submission of policy to the intellectual market place requires special exertions and imaginative treatment on the part of the politician. He must explain and justify the policy to an alert, inquisitive, critical, well-informed group. Public policy must meet a test of approval by what Rosenau describes as the opinion-makers.[14] The people so categorized perform a very important function. Rosenau says that we cannot expect opinion-makers to achieve ideological consensus, nor will their considerations of public policy issues be at all coordinated.[15] The role of the opinion-makers is particularly essential because they alert the electorate by reviewing, debating, and disseminating ideas, particularly when they strongly approve or disapprove of the objectives of a policy. They play a significant role in bringing the alternatives to the attention of the public which for many reasons (i.e. apathy, lack of time, ignorance, prejudice) is less intensively involved. Opinion-makers, not more than one or two per cent of the population, may more effectively than the government direct the spotlight on a public issue.

Since public approval or support is ultimately one of the strongest checks on the government's power, the chief executive must realize that he "cannot move too far ahead of public sentiment, else he will be checked in his course." [16] We should recognize, however, that public opinion on most general issues is a highly unstable and fluid force which cannot be accurately described as a barrier to administration policy. It remains the responsibility of the leadership constantly to solidify the slowly yet continually shifting mass of opinion.

The occasions when government is unsuccessful in winning public approval for its policies deserve careful analysis. We may find that the techniques employed to gain understanding and support are totally inadequate. Or perhaps such complicating factors as deep hatred and suspicion of the leadership, myth-making or ideological blindness, or even some unrelated or unaccountable influence may create an immunity to logical analysis or effective utilization of readily available factual information. When this happens, the educative process is hampered. On such occasions democracy may be faced with its most dangerous moments, as Walter Lippmann and George W. Kennan have pointed out. However, it is not my belief that public blindness or stubbornness impede the effective formulation of American foreign policy as much as these critics have on occasion asserted.

It is true, of course, that most foreign policy problems are highly complex, involving questions which are outside the day-to-day experiences of the ordinary citizen. At times presidential leadership is tempted to follow the path of least resistance. As a result, what should be the responsible analysis of policy alternatives sometimes degenerates into sloganeering. This may occur without the conscious recognition of the official spokesmen involved. Such terms as "policy of containment" or "communist threat" were employed originally with reference to specific situations. Because they aroused emotional reactions in support of policies which the administration wished to pursue, they were overused and misused and thus became merely vain slogans. By deliberately playing upon the fear of communism, for example, successive administrations could more easily win support for foreign aid policies. Reference to communist expansionism became a refrain which proved to be a disarmingly simple technique to win public support. The excessive employment of a certain slogan, however, may have reverse results. Its automatic and continued use may result in an immunity to appeals for support. This has already occurred with reference to foreign aid appropriations.

There are situations, some more than others, that require more positive leadership and action by the government before a degree of public understanding will be created. If the leadership concludes that there is insufficient awareness and considerable confusion about a certain policy, it must intensify its efforts to win the public's attention and support. But an infallible formula for effective measurement of public awareness or sentiment has not yet been found. Evaluations of public opinion most frequently are based on the following criteria: the polls, the views expressed in the mass media with special attention devoted to the editorials and the syndicated writers, the views of interest groups, and the opinions of various elites.

Quincy Wright summarizes this by saying: "Leadership is always aware of its need of popular support and the public is always aware of its need for intelligent leadership." [17] This observation, however, tells us nothing about the influence of public opinion on leadership. Even a cursory examination of the evidence available demonstrates that the connecting links between popular sentiment and government response are often quite tenuous and can only be surmised, not measured. Further generalizations depend on such variables as the human dilemmas and the subjective, as well as objective responses of a president. On no occasion are one hundred units of public sympathy, demand, or enthusiasm going to equal one hundred units of leadership response or inaction. It is a problem which challenges our comprehension; and this is only a facet of the larger quest for comprehension of the role of the presidency which has received much attention in the literature of the last decade.[18]

Finally, what then can be said about the relationship between leadership and public opinion in a democracy? We must remember that there is an important distinction between democratic practice and theory. Lord Lindsay, commenting on this dichotomy, states: "There is always a terrible gulf between the fine and elevating theories about democracy which we read in books on political theory and the actual facts of politics." [19] Democratic theory has usually assumed that the citizen makes rational political judgments. The theory assumes, Berelson writes, that the citizen "is expected to have arrived at his principles by reason and to have considered rationally the implications and alleged consequences of the alternative proposals of the contending parties." [20]

Though classical political thought indicates that we can expect man to be rational and politically inclined most of the time, the study of political behavior does not verify this assumption. James Bryce recognized this inconsistency in 1888, perhaps expressing it somewhat harshly. "How little solidity and substance there is in the political or social beliefs of nineteen persons out of every twenty. These beliefs, when examined, mostly resolve themselves into two or three prejudices and aversions, two or three prepossessions for a particular party or section of a party, two or three phrases or catchwords suggesting or embodying arguments which the man who repeats them has not analyzed." [21] Several studies published in recent years show the lack of public awareness of foreign policy issues. In Gabriel Almond's view only a small group is well enough informed to participate effectively in an evaluation of foreign policy. At best, Almond writes, the "general public" will react to various stimuli, the extent of the reaction depending upon the alertness and knowledgeability involved. [22]

Even more significant than the lack of information is the role of apathy. In the view of one observer, substantial evidence has been made available which indicates that "man, far from becoming a self-impelled political being is, in fact, rather apathetic about political matters." [23] And what is apathy? Professor Nisbet refers to a definition by a zoologist who says that apathy "is a characteristic response of any living organism to stimuli which are too intense or too complicated for it to cope with." [24] This definition poignantly stresses the dilemma of the individual living in a violent and incomprehensible world; the citizen in our society is confronted with so many harassing problems that he cannot even attempt to understand. Judge Learned Hand, writing about voting, once said: "The simplest problems which come up from day to day seem to me quite unanswerable as soon as I try to get below the surface." [25]

It is ironical, however, that while we deplore political apathy, we must recognize that political leadership would soon be paralyzed by indecisiveness if the mass of the citizenry demonstrated permanent political consciousness. Edward A. Shils remarks on this point: "Democracy requires the occasional political participation of most of its citizenry some of the time, and a moderate and dim perceptiveness —as if from the corner of the eye—the rest of the time. It could not function if politics and the state of the social order were always on everyone's mind." [26] V. O. Key feels that a healthy democracy requires the presence of a small corps of political activists and opinion elite. He notes that "the policies of a democratic order depend ultimately on the outlooks and concerns of the more active citizenry rather than on mass opinion." This view leads him to the conclusion "that those who blame mass opinion for our ills hang the wrong villain." [27] The opinion elite, composed of a very small segment of the public, influences the views of the leadership and helps to formulate the consensus of opinion which will guide governmental policy. Public opinion does not assist in the task of finding the specific solution in the field of foreign policy. Nevertheless, "acceptability to popular opinion is certainly a factor in the conduct of foreign policy by our government." Marshall persuasively summarizes this problem when he writes that public opinion is important "in setting bounds to the area of maneuver available to those charged with responsibility." [28] This is especially true when a leader must decide on a course of action before he has had the opportunity to solicit public support.

What then can be said about the relation between leadership and public opinion in a democracy? Lester Pearson believes that "there is nothing in the theory of democratic government which requires a public servant to speak or vote or act contrary to his own judgment of the nation's best interests." [29] However, the politician must consider the acceptability of the decision that he has to make, so that he can proceed to adapt "his timing and method of presentation." Arthur Schlesinger, Jr. summarizes in one sentence the challenge of leadership in a democracy. Raising the question "Why does a statesman make a decision?", Schlesinger notes that "the decision is generally the result of an accommodation between his own views of what is wise and the felt pressures upon him as to what is possible." [30]

Walt Rostow comments that "while the American public is not inclined to follow blindly the President's lead, his view is a powerful element in the equation which determines public opinion." Moreover, he points out, the American people are "inclined to give him [the President] a considerable latitude and to be influenced significantly by his assessment of external events and their meaning for the national interest." [31]

Professor Key formulates an important hypothesis: only a very small proportion of the public will pay much attention to specific issues, but a larger percentage will have an interest in the broader issues. Key concludes that it is a "basic supposition of democracy that in one way or another governmental action should parallel popular wishes or at least meet with popular acceptance." [32] This limitation still leaves the government a very wide choice of action. We recognize that there are many influences which may affect public opinion, but political leadership itself serves as a most significant factor in the molding of popular attitudes. Professor Key emphasizes this responsibility when he writes that "it is as much the duty of government to seek to change a public opinion that it believes to be in error as it is to respond to an opinion that it judges to be in the public interest." [33]

Harold Lasswell defines the distinguishing mark of democracy as the two-way connection between opinion and policy. "Democratic government acts upon public opinion, and public opinion acts openly and continually upon government." [34] Morgenthau suggests "the degree to which the President is willing to execute the foreign policies his advisers suggest depends upon his estimate of the public support his policies will command." [35]

Two spokesmen in particular, one British and the other American, raise their voices to protest against the ineptitude of the modern democratic state in adequately facing the challenges confronting democracies during the twentieth century. Walter Lippmann, as early as 1925 in *The Phantom Public* and in *The Public Philosophy* published in 1955, protests against "the popular view that in a democracy public men are the servants . . . of the people." [36] Lippmann's thesis is that the responsibility of a political leader must be to his office and not to the people; he also argues "that the prevailing public opinion had been destructively wrong at the critical junctures." [37]

Similar arguments may be found in the writings of the British historian A. L. Rowse of Oxford University. He has identified the three essential pillars of democracy as leadership, propaganda, and education. He stresses that the most important of these pillars is leadership. [38] Having lived most of their lives in a world enveloped by chaos, both Rowse and Lippmann deplore the inadequacies and the devitalization of democratic political leadership. Rowse, writing with some passion about the role of leadership before the Second World War, exclaims: "And, anyhow what are the political leaders for? Do we employ them to fall for the enemies of their country, to put across to us the lies they are such fools as to believe? Not at all: the proper function of political leaders is precisely *not* to be taken in, but to warn us." [39] There is the inherent assumption that if the "warnings" which did not materialize had been issued, majority opinion would have supported a drastic revision of foreign policy vis-a-vis Nazi Germany.

Is it correct to conclude that by action and leadership government "can to some degree elicit the pressures" which will propel it in the direction it has chosen to go? [40] Many have wrestled with this question. Interestingly, a Scottish philosopher, James Mill (1773-1836), and the foreign-relations chief of the United States Senate, J. William Fulbright, have expressed comparable ideas. James Mill wrote, "When various conclusions are, with their evidence, presented with equal care and equal skill, there is a moral certainty, though some few may be misguided, that the greatest number will judge right, and that the greatest force of evidence, wherever it is, will produce the greatest impression." [41]

Senator Fulbright has observed that "If men are often irrational in their political behavior, it does not follow that they are *always* irrational and, what is more important, it does not follow that they are incapable of reason." [42] In his view, man is capable of making rational moral choices involving political goals, but he lacks the capacity to achieve these goals without effective political leadership. Senator Fulbright expresses this thought in the following metaphor: "The experience of modern times shows us that when the passengers take over the navigation of the ship it is likely to go on the rocks. This does not mean that their chosen destination is the wrong one or that an expert would have made a better choice, but only that they are unlikely to get there without the navigator's guidance." [43]

Acknowledgement that the public is prone to mood impulses from time to time, or is "vulnerable to subjectivity," does not imply irrationality. The criticism that a policy lacks rationality more often than not simply indicates disapproval of the means proposed for dealing with a situation. Particularly with reference to foreign policy, the criticism that a policy lacks rationality does not necessarily mean that it is absurd or that it was formulated without reason. An irrational policy depends heavily upon those influences which appeal to the emotions, but this does not automatically make a policy irrational. And the rational approach does not have to be devoid of emotion before we can characterize it as being reasonable.

The challenge of democratic leadership is constantly to improve the climate of opinion by clearly delineating policy alternatives and by equipping every citizen with all relevant facts within the limits permitted by national security. It is a truism that formulation of foreign policy in a democracy is difficult. But if the atmosphere permits rational discussion of alternatives and the government upholds a basic but infrequently mentioned freedom—that of freedom from victimization of governmental propaganda—then we have the optimum setting for decision-making in a democracy.

Chapter II

THE SHADOW OF A CRISIS

After his first inauguration Franklin D. Roosevelt was primarily concerned with domestic problems. According to James Farley, however, the President "was much more interested in foreign affairs than he indicated in public utterances and press conferences." [1]

As early as February 1934, Hamilton Fish Armstrong pointed out to the President that as the spokesman for the "citadel of democracy" he had the obligation at "an early opportunity to re-affirm, publicly and emphatically, your belief in liberalism and democracy." "I believe," Armstrong added, "that abroad the effect would be reinvigorating and that it would serve the long-range interests of the United States. The peoples of Europe needed to be reminded that the most powerful nation in the world has not yet decided that the only alternatives to choose between are communist dictatorship or fascist dictatorship." [2]

Although Roosevelt made public references to the crisis developing overseas, there was a surprising discrepancy between his public utterances and his private views. [3] As a result—at least in part—his administration suffered several resounding defeats at the hands of the isolationists when the Johnson Bill was passed in 1934, when the First Neutrality Law was enacted in August 1935, and when our adherence to the World Court protocol was turned down by the Senate in the same year. Selig Adler in his excellent study of American isolationism stresses that while the President was unhappy about these developments, he "made no real effort to brake the rolling isolationist bandwagon." He said then, as he was to say on many later occasions, that the time was not yet ripe for action. [4]

That Roosevelt's public utterances were not always identical with his private views is substantiated by his correspondence with Colonel House. In an early letter, April 1935, the President expressed his regret to House that he had no one like him "to fulfill for me the splendid missions which you carried out in Europe before we got into the war—but there is only one *you* and I know of no other." [5] He also indicated that he was greatly disturbed about events in Europe; "perhaps more than I should be," he added. There is no doubt that Roosevelt appreciated the full significance of the announcement of compulsory military training in Germany made public on March 10, 1935.

11

Nor can we question his appreciation that in a world torn between communism and fascism America's efforts to stabilize herself gave hope to democratic nations everywhere.

President Roosevelt admitted that he had considered several methods by which the United States could best use its influence to stop the rapidly increasing armaments race, but he rejected various alternatives "for the principal reason that I fear any suggestion on our part would meet with the same kind of chilly, half-contemptuous reception on the other side as an appeal would have met in July or August 1914." [6]

Particularly interesting is the fact that eleven months before Germany denounced the Locarno Pacts and occupied the Rhineland President Roosevelt asked Colonel House to consider the feasibility of a plan which entailed some form of joint military and naval action against Germany. He suggested the complete blockade of Germany's borders and ports and considered the possibility of American involvement." "Such a blockade," he confided to House, "Would raise for us the question of its effectiveness. If we found it was an effective blockade, as a mater of fact, recognition of the blockade by us would obviously follow. This, after all, is not a boycott nor an economic sanction, but in effect it is the same thing. A boycott or sanction would not be recognized by us without Congressional action but a blockade would fall under the Executive's power after establishment of the fact. I advance this thought because rumor has come to me that something along this line may be discussed at Stresa." [7]

Five months later in another letter to Colonel House the President expressed his objections to the views of some Congressmen and Senators "who are suggesting wild-eyed measures to keep us out of war." The tone of this letter indicates clearly that he was in sharp disagreement with those who "imagine that if the civilization of Europe is about to destroy itself through international strife, it might just as well go ahead and do it and that the United States can stand idly by." [8] The principal reason Roosevelt kept silent was not the possible negative reception to his proposals, but the complete absence of support for such suggestions at home. Many able and sympathetic studies have indicated that privately he was an internationalist, while publicly he continued "to work with or toy with the isolationists." [8]

The question of whether or not President Roosevelt "was as much a reflector of public opinion as he was a maker of it" [9] has been much debated; in my judgment, during the thirties, particularly with reference to Europe, he was much more the former than the latter.

While the President was privately expressing concern about the developments in Europe, at home he was faced with serious legislative problems which had brought the New Deal almost to a stalemate. 1935 was the year F.D.R. was confronted with the unconstitutionality of the National Recovery Administration and the year the Supreme Court made front-page headlines. It was the time when Father Coughlin and Huey Long were stingingly critical of the President. This was the period, as Arthur Schlesinger, Jr. has stated, when "the legacy of the First New Deal was . . . fragmenting in a bewildering way." [10]

The President did utilize some public occasions to refer to aggressive totalitarian forces overseas, and, in so far as he felt that he could safely do so, he tried to circumscribe the efforts of Congress to limit the Executive powers in foreign affairs. For example, Langer and Gleason point out that while Roosevelt did not disagree with the content of the Neutrality Act of 1935, he could appreciate that this measure was establishing a dangerous precedent by requiring an arms embargo on both an attacking and a defending country. On August 31, 1935, in a statement prepared for the signing of that law, Roosevelt said "it is conceivable that situations may arise in which the wholly inflexible provisions of Section I of this Act may have exactly the opposite effect from that which was intended." [12]

At the outset it seemed as if the 1936 election campaign would be a tough struggle. Roosevelt's prestige was low, the opposition was confident, and a Gallup poll predicted a bare majority for the President. [13] During this campaign F.D.R. delivered a foreign policy address at Chautauqua, New York, on August 14th, intended to persuade the isolationists that he was in sympathy with them; he needed their votes. Even Basil Rauch, who wrote a study of the foreign relations of the Roosevelt administration to rebut the thesis put forward by Charles Beard that F.D.R. maneuvered the United States into the Second World War, admits this. Because the President said "We shun political commitments which entangle us in foreign wars; we avoid connection with the political activities of the League of Nations," the speech was in part an appeal to the isolationists. However, he added the following warnings, "We are not isolationists except in so far as we seek to isolate ourselves completely from war. Yet we must remember that so long as war exists on earth there will be some danger that even the Nation which most ardently desires peace may be drawn into war." [14]

It soon became evident that appeals for peace accompanied by promises to avoid entanglement were not retarding the inevitable march toward international involvement. Subsequent to the German repudiation of the Versailles Treaty and the Ethiopian crisis in 1935, the world witnessed German reoccupation of the Rhineland, the beginning of the Civil War in Spain, the establishment of the Berlin-Rome Axis and the signing of the Anti-Comintern Pact between Germany and Japan in 1936. The Third Neutrality Law was signed by the President in May, 1937, despite his opposition to its inflexible provisions and his attempt to prevent further Congressional encroachment of executive powers in foreign affairs.

At the outbreak of hostilities between Japan and China in July, 1937, the British government asked the United States and France to join her in formulating proposals which might end the fighting. Cordell Hull rejected this proposal because anything resembling joint action with Britain inevitably aroused the fears and animosity of the isolationist elements in the United States. Hull also thought that joint action would serve no useful purpose "unless it embraced a real show of force." In October 1937, however, it was decided to send a delegation under the leadership of Norman H. Davis to the Brussels Conference called to consider measures which could be taken with regard to the fighting in China.[15]

After consulting with the American delegates Anthony Eden was troubled: "In a message to the Foreign Office I summed up our conclusion, that the Americans attached importance to the Conference as an influence for educating their public. They did not know what step they might be able to take next, but they hoped the Conference would gain more energetic public support for them. Evidently it was all to be a slow business, but Britain had no choice."[16]

The conference did not take place at a propitious time. It is highly unlikely that opinion would have supported collective sanctions, even though Americans were somewhat more willing to take action in regard to the Orient than in disciplining the dictators in Europe. When Davis and Eden discussed the possibility of denying credits or refusing recognition of Japanese conquests, Under-Secretary of State Sumner Welles signified that the United States was not willing to go that far. In his memoirs Eden also makes note of the role of public opinion on the occasion of the attack on the *Panay* and the British warships off the coast of China. To his disappointment, separate notes of protest were sent by the American and British governments. British policy was under suspicion of attempting to entangle the United States, Eden observes:

"There was a strong isolationist lobby, which the United States Government had to take into account, even though they did not share its views. The dilemma was expressed by Mr. Hull, himself certainly circumspect:

" 'While advocating international co-operation at all times, we were faced with the extremely delicate task of being careful not to present and urge measures in such numbers as to alarm the people and precipitate isolation as an acute political issue in the nation.' " [17]

There is some evidence, then, that on a number of important occasions the U. S. government dragged its feet when cooperation was possible, or acted unilaterally because of the feeling that public support was lacking. However, at approximately the same time the President was giving a visiting French statesman the impression "that he was intent on arousing the American public and on developing international cooperation in the effort to save the peace." [18] Just how adept Roosevelt was in carrying out these twin tasks remains open to question.

Increasingly worried about the growth of isolationist sentiment, Hull and Norman Davis suggested that the President deliver a speech prior to the Brussels Conference. They felt that he should stress the importance of international cooperation and that he should speak in a large city recognized as a citadel of isolationism, Chicago. This was to be the famous "Quarantine Address," the first draft of which was prepared in the State Department by Norman Davis; but this draft made no reference to the "quarantine" idea, although it did include the phrase "war is a contagion." [19] Hull himself states he had no idea that the reference to "quarantine" was inserted shortly before delivery. [20]

In some respects the theme of Roosevelt's October speech was a familiar one. In the aforementioned Chautauqua address, for example, the President said "that even the nation which most ardently desires peace may be drawn into war." In his Chicago speech the President elaborated on this theme. He said that the United States had to look to the future because we were living in a world where some nations were spending 30 to 50 per cent of their national income for armaments, while we were spending only 11 per cent. He stressed the point that "the peace, the freedom, the security of ninety per cent of the population of the world is being jeopardized by the remaining ten per cent who are threatening a breakdown of all international order and law" and that this was a situation which concerned everyone. He reiterated that he was determined "to pursue a policy of peace." The President was, however, much more frank about the long-run implications of the "reign of terror and international lawlessness" which existed in the world. Referring to the "recent systematic violation of treaties, the indiscriminate bombing of civilians, the waging of undeclared war," he now ventured to warn the American people that "if those things come to pass in other parts of the world, let no one imagine that America will escape, that America may expect mercy, that this Western Hemisphere will not be attacked." [21] Reflecting on this speech, Roosevelt wrote in July 1941, "To meet that epidemic of world lawlessness I proposed that the community of nations throughout the world act the same as communities do when 'an epidemic of physical disease starts to spread,' namely, join in a quarantine 'in order to protect the health of the community against the spread of the disease.' " [22]

These remarks stirred a hornet's nest and the stings of the multitudinous isolationists had an almost paralyzing effect on the man who dared to disturb them. Reaction against the quarantine idea was quick and violent, and Roosevelt observed that his suggestions "fell upon deaf ears—even hostile and resentful ears." He was acused of warmongering, and the speech was "ridiculed as a nervous search 'under the bed' for dangers of war which did not exist." The key word in the campaign to win public support for international cooperation had been "gradualness." [23] Now the administration unwittingly offered itself as a target for the bitter counterattacks of the isolationist spokesmen.

During the press conference the day after the Chicago speech reporters naturally tried to ascertain the meaning and the implication of the word "quarantine," but the President was reluctant to amplify his remarks. When asked by one correspondent whether he was speaking "of something more than moral indignation," whether he was preparing the way for collaborative action, he replied that the speech itself was a step in this direction. Asked about a possible resort to sanctions, the President responded, "They are out of the window," and added that this applied to conferences as well. Remaining calm in face of the critical questions fired by the press corps, he called their attention to the concluding sentence of his speech, "America actively engages in the search for peace," and rejected the implication this was in any way contrary to our policy of neutrality. When a reporter referred to the *London Times* comment that the speech was the expression of an attitude without a program, the President bluntly replied, "It is an attitude and it does not outline a program but says we are looking for a program." [24]

Quite obviously shaken by the negative impact his words had had on public opinion, Roosevelt responded to a question at a subsequent press conference on October eighth by saying, "No, I cannot say anything further than what I said Wednesday morning because I haven't talked to anybody since then."

Two excerpts from the many letters received by the President are typical of negative comments to the Quarantine Address.

"Mr. President, the mothers who have watched their boys grow into manhood, watched them strive to become useful citizens, are not going to let them go into foreign lands to fight. We had enough of that before. No more can we say there is any glory in laying down one's life for his country, no not when we are called upon to fight someone's elses' battle." [25]

"My dear Mr. President: After reading your Chicago speech on international policy a great many of us are asking ourselves if we are headed now for a repetition of Wilson's folly." [26]

Roosevelt was aware of the confused reaction to the speech from his perusal of different newspaper editorials, and he said in his press conference on October sixth "there are no two of them which agree." Not all the papers were critical, however. *The Oregonian* on October 7, 1937, wrote: "President Roosevelt's speech scales heights. The thoughts to which he gives voice cannot fail to strike a responsive chord in the hearts of all true Americans." [27] Ironically, praise also came from unexpected quarters. Westbrook Pegler's headline for his regular column "Fair Enough" read "Roosevelt May Have Said Just What was Needed to Avert New World War." "The President's speech on the hoodlum nations was a shocker," thought Pegler, but he was glad that Roosevelt had "upped and busted them one." "Both Mussolini and Hitler have openly declared their contempt for democracy, and it is surely no mistake, in view of their oft-expressed detestation of American ideals, for the American President to let it be said for the sake of the record, that the loathing is mutual, if no more so. . . . No country is safe which isn't able and ready to protect itself." [28]

It has often been assumed that Roosevelt was overwhelmed by the dissident response to his speech and that this criticism explains his later reluctance to speak frankly on the issue of American assistance to the European democracies. Although the President announced seven days after the Chicago speech that sanctions would not be contemplated, his private correspondence demonstrates that there was no retreat from his previous position. He wrote to Colonel House that he had expected more criticism and added "I verily believe that as time goes on we can slowly but surely make people realize that war will be a greater danger to us if we close all the doors and windows than if we go out in the street and use our influence to curb the riot." [29]

Two months later he informed a family friend that the nation wanted peace, but not the kind of peace ". . . which means definite danger to us at home in the days to come," and the sense of the letter suggested that the country could not afford to settle for peace at any price.[30] Perhaps he was heartened to some extent by reports from personal observers that the people had not reacted as negatively as a *Philadelphia Inquirer* poll and editorial comment had indicated. Raymond Leslie Buell reported to James Roosevelt that he was pleasantly surprised to hear enthusiastic support for the President's speech at a Memphis conference attended by dirt farmers, labor leaders, and editors from the South and the Middle West.[31] Despite these reports and his own feelings about the threat to world peace presented by the Nazi menace, the President knew that public opinion was not with him; and some time was to pass before he again made a concerted effort to persuade Americans to support a firmer policy against the aggressor. To what extent he was compelled by pressure from within as well as from outside the administration to renew his struggle for public support is a question that will be examined in detail in the following chapters.

The explanation for the poor reception of the Quarantine Address is threefold. First, this was a period of the most rampant isolationism, highlighted by the 1935 revelations of the Nye Committee, the Ludlow Amendment which was only narrowly defeated in January 1938, and the new neutrality law which was passed by a vast majority. In 1937, public opinion polls showed that a large majority of the American people thought our entry into the First World War had been a mistake. Secondly, after occasional public pleas for peace, accompanied by guarantees of nonentanglement, the call for international collaboration against the aggressor nations left the American people in a state of shock. Thirdly, given this background, the occasion for the speech was not favorable because the President's prestige had reached a low ebb, not only because of the Supreme Court issue, but also because the economy had taken a downward turn.

Hadley Cantril once suggested that "by and large, public opinion does not anticipate emergencies; it only reacts to them." [32] And the public opinion data for the 1938-1939 period bears this out. News of

Hitler's occupation of Austria and the Munich crisis seemed to have a considerable impact on public opinion. In March of 1939, 66 per cent expressed support of the sale of military equipment to England and France, while only 34 per cent expressed this sentiment in September of 1938.[33] However, Congress was not in step with this change of attitude; the President really wanted the repeal of the Neutrality Act, but because of the strength of the isolationist bloc in the Senate he asked only for the revocation of the arms embargo. Even this request was not supported by the Congress. In the fall of 1938 President Roosevelt began to pay more attention to problems of national defense. He planned to build up our military strength, but he wished to do this without provoking too much public controversy. The Democrats had not fared well in the Congressional elections of 1938, and the isolationists remained a powerful group in the Congress. The President therefore felt that he could not go beyond the proposals for strengthening our national defense and for building closer defensive ties in this hemisphere. He optimistically counted on some support from the isolationists for this particular program.

Two books concerned in part with this period, and which analyze the administration's approach to the international crisis of 1938-1939, conclude that Roosevelt was reluctant to place the issues and the alternatives of policy before the American people. Langer and Gleason gently raise some basic questions, while Donald F. Drummond frankly concludes that we adopted a policy of appeasement at this time. Writing about the President's view, Langer and Gleason said: "The question has often been raised and debated why, if the President was aware of the dangers inherent in the European situation after Munich, he did not state them publicly and use his tremendous influence and prestige to induce a change in American opinion."[34] The authors conclude that the answer to this question is a complicated one because the administration, although well aware of the danger of war, did not envision the possibility of future American intervention. Therefore, the problem was not one of preparing public opinion for such an eventuality, but was instead one of bolstering American defenses and building up an arsenal upon which the European democracies could draw. "This," Langer and Gleason observe, "Mr. Roosevelt apparently hoped to accomplish without provoking too much public controversy, avoidance of which seemed to him at the time to be absolutely essential."[35] Donald F. Drummond is somewhat less charitable in his observations. He suggests that the President did not fully appreciate the importance of Munich and observes that "the American government dabbled in appeasement through most of 1938." [36] Drummond further draws the conclusion that "American foreign policy between the middle of 1938 and the spring of 1939 was caution mixed with confusion." [37]

Basil Rauch, on the other hand, presents sound evidence that Roosevelt fully appreciated the dangers of appeasement and explains how the timing of Roosevelt's interventions in the Munich crisis gave rise to the later accusation that the President "implicated himself in Champerlain's appeasement of Hitler at Munich." [38] Nevertheless, it is true, as Drummond points out, that Roosevelt was continually "balancing one statement against another" and thereby, cancelled any positive gains that had been made in winning the support of public opinion for a more active foreign policy.

A good example of this is the President's bitter and repeated denial of his alleged statement at an executive session of the Military Affairs Committee, January 31, 1939, that the American frontier was on the Rhine. Asked at a press conference whether he thought that this catch phrase summed up the situation, the President replied: "Of course not." [39] On the other hand, one of the important themes of the annual message to the Congress, delivered on January 4, 1939, was the attempt to awaken appreciation of the fact that our spiritual frontier was the Rhine. In this speech he emphasized the need for a close relationship with other democracies. "God-fearing democracies," he said, "cannot forever let pass, without effective protest, acts of aggression against sister nations—acts which automatically undermine all of us." He stressed, however, that there would be no intervention with arms "to prevent acts of aggression."

The point is that, after severe criticism in the press and attacks by isolationists in and out of Congress, the President seemed to hastily retreat from the dramatic (in the context of the times) statement attributed to him. Yet, despite his most vehement denials of any responsibility for this statement, a little more than a year later he delineated in the clearest way what he had been saying to the Military Affairs Committee. Addressing members of the Business Advisory Council on May 23, 1940, the President said that he had told the Committee over a year before that there would be a war and, he continued, "not that 'our frontier was on the Rhine' but that the continued existence of, for example, Finland, or the Baltic States, or the Scandinavian nations — did have a pretty definite relationship to the defense of the United States. And there was a most awful howl of protest all over the country, as you know, at that time." [40]

CHAPTER III

AFTER MUNICH

Privately, the President had always recognized the danger to peace, and after Munich he was more anxious than ever to lend encouragement to the democracies. He now felt that the time had come to take a more active stand against the Axis and to let the struggle for domestic reforms take second place. One of the most effective ways in which America could help the Allies would be to repeal the all-embracing arms embargo and to replace it with a discriminatory embargo against aggressor nations.

President Roosevelt spoke of the Munich agreement in his annual message to the Congress in 1939, saying that "a war which threatened to envelop the world in flames has been averted; but it has become increasingly clear that world peace is not assured." Here for the first time is an indirect reference to the fact that security might mean something more than the repelling of enemy soldiers from American beachheads. The President spoke forthrightly and directly to the isolationists who represented the "Fortress America" concept.

"There comes a time in the affairs of men when they must prepare to defend, not their homes alone, but the tenets of faith and humanity on which their churches, their governments and their very civilization are founded. The defense of religion, of democracy and of good faith among nations is all the same fight. To save one we must now make up our minds to save all."

He continued: "We, no more than other nations, can afford to be surrounded by the enemies of our faith and our humanity," and he also emphasized the need for a strong defense by stating "we have learned that survival cannot be guaranteed by arming after the attack begins for there is new range and speed to offense." Lawless acts against other nations must be protested; otherwise such acts may "undermine all of us." Making once again the same generalized reference to action as in the Quarantine Address, the President said:

"The mere fact that we rightly decline to intervene with arms to prevent acts of aggression does not mean that we must act as if there were no aggression at all. Words may be futile, but war is not the only means of commanding a decent respect for the opinions of mankind. There are many methods short of war but stronger and more effective than mere words, of bringing home to aggressor governments the aggregate sentiments of our own people."

Roosevelt stressed that a state of readiness was the best way to discourage aggression and noted that the "innate decency of mankind" had not protected the unprepared during the last eight years. In conclusion, the President said that he realized that there were still many problems which had to be solved on the domestic front; but he warned that "events across the sea have made it increasingly clear to the American people that dangers within are less to be feared than dangers from without."

The response to the President's address across the nation, and particularly in the Congress, emphasized the divided views on the subject of neutrality. Again Roosevelt was dismayed by the strong reaction to his speech; he decided that the best way to fight was to withdraw from the scene, letting his Congressional lieutenants wage the battle for revision. When he was questioned in his news conference about his reference to "means other than war to let the aggressor nations know our sentiments," he said that he had no specific actions in mind at present.[1]

However, just as the President wished to give the impression of remaining in the background, an unfortunate leak occurred in the Senate Military Affairs Committee.[2] The word was out that Roosevelt had said at a meeting of this committee that "our frontier in the battle of democracies versus fascism" was on the Rhine. President Roosevelt referred to this statement as a "deliberate lie," but it was to haunt him for a long while and was especially embarrassing at this time because of his desire to minimize his own role in the neutrality revision fight. Anxious to set the record straight, Roosevelt deemphasized the criticism the statement aroused and took up the question in a press conference. He pointed out that the independent military and economic existence of democracies outside the hemisphere would help to protect the democracies of this hemisphere. Listing a number of European and Middle Eastern countries, the President said that "we have a continuing interest in their remaining free and independent." He reminded the reporters that Austria and Czechoslovakia must already be subtracted from this list of countries, and that Hungary, Yugoslavia, Bulgaria and Romania were not as independent as they once had been. When asked how the phrase "frontier on the Rhine" might have originated, Roosevelt replied: "Very simple. It is the kind of term that could scare the American people, politically, and out of which they [the opposition] could make political capital."[3]

Perhaps if the President had been able to exert a little more leadership at this point, his warnings would have been heeded. But he was in a precarious position: first, there was the strategy of restraint to win the fight for revision of the Neutrality Act; second, with every word of warning he let fall, he was accused of warmongering.[4]

There is no question that there was considerable resentment of the administration at this time. This feeling stemmed not just from recent administrative action in the foreign field, but was a residue of many New Deal measures. Rauch refers to the "accumulated distempers of the six strenuous New Deal years."[5] The President, who was usually magnificent in handling the press, showed the strain of constant attack and criticism when he lashed out at the press on February 3, 1939. Emphasizing the point that there was nothing new about our foreign policy, he told the assembled reporters that "a great many people, some members of the House, some members of the Senate and quite a number of newspaper owners, are deliberately putting before the American people a deliberate misrepresentation of facts—deliberate."[6] He stressed that our foreign policy had not changed and was not going to change. With these statements, however, the President, as on previous occasions, weakened a strong position which had won the attention of the public.

In his February press conference, Roosevelt summarized the principles of our policy in the following way:

Number 1: "We are against any entangling alliances, obviously.

Number 2: "We are in favor of the maintenance of world trade for everybody—all nations—including ourselves.

Number 3: "We are in complete sympathy with any and every effort made to reduce or limit armaments.

Number 4: "As a Nation—as American people—we are sympathetic with the peaceful maintenance of political, economic and social independence of all nations in the world."[7]

This succinct statement of our foreign policy aims did not satisfy those people who supported the Allied cause and who appreciated the nature of the totalitarian menace. They were becoming exceedingly restless about the lack of leadership of public opinion. One of these was Clyde Eagleton, Professor at New York University, who wrote to Dr. Stanley K. Hornbeck, Political Advisor to the State Department on February 16, 1939:

"[The] American people have been confused through irresponsible leadership and . . . would welcome a clear statement, and would follow it with relief. In various meetings we discussed this, and everywhere I have found this belief. And when I ask who could furnish such leadership, the answer is always: 'Only the President could do it; if only he would give a fireside chat!' It has been my experience that when the matter is explained to people, they turn against the policy in the neutrality legislation. How far they may be willing to go after that varies; but they can readily be convinced that the policy is wrong." [8]

Roosevelt obviously had accurate information, but he was not using it to alert the American people as some thought he should. On February 18, 1939, preparing for one of his departures from Warm Springs he was quoted as saying, "I'll be back in the fall, if we don't have a war." In connection with this particular quotation the President indicated his approval of an editorial entitled "The Collective Pronoun" that appeared in the *Washington Post*, by making it available at a subsequent press conference. It is quoted here in part because of the special effort made by Roosevelt to focus public attention on it.

"'I'll be back in the fall, if we don't have a war.' These words, spoken by the President to the group assembled at Warm Springs to see him off for Washington, were seemingly wholly unpremediated. Actually it is proper to surmise that serious consideration preceded their utterance. No one knows better than the President that his office makes his most casual public observation subject to interpretation as a matter of national policy. And no President was ever more skillful than Mr. Roosevelt in making the most of every opportunity to give a positive direction to public thinking on important issues.

"Most Americans realize today that the sweep of events has now brought Europe to the very verge of war. What is insufficiently realized is the tremendous implication of the impending catastrophe for every citizen of this country." [9]

Robert E. Osgood sketched the dilemma of the President clearly and accurately:

"Roosevelt, like his cautious Secretary of State, Cordell Hull, was acutely conscious of the force of traditional attitudes toward American foreign policy and, perhaps, too little aware of the transformation of the American outlook being wrought under the impact of revolutionary circumstances. Consequently, he defended America's step-by-step involvement in the world struggle for power too much in terms of neutrality, nonintervention, and altruism at a time when these traditional considerations were becoming increasingly irrelevant to the real issues which troubled the American public. Thus in order to appease an isolationist minority he muddled the public's perception of the hardheaded case for American aid to the anti-Fascist powers and weakened its will to act upon that perception. Whether this was an inevitable result of necessary domestic political expediency is another matter." [10]

A. A. Berle, Jr. summarized this crucial issue effectively when he emphasized America's Hamlet-like role in a memorandum to the President on April 24, 1939, "Americans want two inconsistent things at once: to stay out of war, and to damn the side they disagree with." [11]

R. Walton Moore touched upon this same point when he wrote to Ambassador Bullitt in Paris on December 27, 1939. The following passage from his letter also stresses the President's problem. "American sympathy for the Allies is very pronounced, but at the same time there is marked increasing opposition to permitting this country to become involved in the European war by anything that may happen. This opposition is based not alone upon consideration of the loss of life and the expense that participation in the war would mean, but even more upon the theory that our Government should occupy an impartial position at the end of the war so as to try to do what is necessary for the peace of the world." [12]

Many of Roosevelt's advisors and close friends were torn by the same doubts and inconsistent views as those of the public. Typical of one type of attitude were the thoughts of Josephus Daniels. In a letter written to the President on September 4, 1939, Daniels expressed the hope that we would be able to maintain peace in our hemisphere. He also wished that a strong stand on our part would bring a quick end to the dictators, as if a hard stare would be sufficient to make them buckle. The reluctance to face the world realistically is alarming:

"Our manifest destiny is on this hemisphere. Above all, our task is to preserve here the best democracy of which mankind is capable and to preserve a standard to which warring countries will resort when their fever of madness has spent itself.

"I follow with the deepest interest all you are doing for peace. I am sure your noble appeals would have had effect if anything could have influenced Hitler and the other dictators. But they believe they now have enough force to dominate the world and nothing can stop them. I have the faith that as in the end Napoleon's and the Kaiser's dream of world dominion was thwarted, a like result will end Hitlerism in our day." [13]

This kind of insipid thinking, typical of much of the advice received by the White House, could not have encouraged the President.

In striking contrast, however, are the clear-cut views of the most outspoken member of the Cabinet. In a speech in Cleveland, December 1938, Harold Ickes had denounced the Germans so bitterly that they filed a protest. He reports that "Welles informed the German Chargé d'Affaires that what I said represented the overwhelming opinion of the people of the United States." Ickes verifies the fact that the President was thoroughly convinced that the European countries were our first line of defense. Referring to a conversation with the President, Ickes notes in his diary on January 29, 1939, "He developed the theory that our first line of defense is really the small countries of Europe that have not yet been overwhelmed by the Nazis. He seriously thinks that if Hitler extends his power over these small countries and then uses the economic weapons that will be his, he will be striking a serious blow at us without even a thought of trying to land a soldier on our shores. There is no doubt that the President is seriously concerned about the situation." [14] Ickes quotes the President as telling the British Ambassador Lord Lothian "that while he [the President] was willing to help all that he could, he would do nothing if Great Britain cringed like a coward."

Ickes, more than anyone else in the Cabinet, was disturbed about the fact that not enough was being done by the government to explain the world crisis and our own role in it to the people. This conversation is reported in his diary, "I told the President that it seemed to me vitally important to educate our own people on the issues involved in this situation. He said that it would be absolutely impossible for him or for me to go on the air and talk to the world as we were talking. The people simply would not believe him. I agreed, but insisted that, notwithstanding this, we had to begin and I suggested that Hull be sent to Chicago or Kansas City to make a speech." [15]

"The people simply would not believe him"—this conviction and the feeling that nothing could be done by the administration to change this response except to await further damaging action by the Axis powers explains the reticence of the President. The chief difference between Roosevelt and the Ickes faction in the Cabinet was that the latter group felt that the people should be made fully aware of America's true interests and needs.

Eight months later Ickes repeated his suggestion to the President. On September 9, 1939, he wrote: "If the President wants to strengthen public sentiment in the country, I believe that he ought to be letting some of us go out to face the people and talk to them about the issues that are involved. I wrote to him to this effect yesterday. We ought to talk neutrality and peace, but we can talk those subjects while pointing out the dangers of Nazism to such a country as ours. I haven't the slightest doubt that if Hitler should smash France and Britain before being bled white, he would next turn his attention to the richest country in the world and therefore the greatest prize of a conqueror, the United States." [16]

The President's own role of standing quietly aside during the Congressional debate on the repeal of mandatory neutrality was imposed as well upon other spokesmen of the administration. The President sent this memorandum to Ickes on September 16, 1939, "You are right about leading the right kind of public opinion in this country. As a matter of practical politics I think it is better for us to withhold any speeches, such as talks to Poles, etc., for just a very short time, i.e. until we get the embargo repeal through. In other words, merely a matter of timing. F.D.R." [17]

All sources of information were, of course, open to the President and he was particularly interested in reports from informed observers traveling around the country. As far back as 1933, Roosevelt suggested to Cornelius Vanderbilt, journalist and lecturer, that he send him occasional comments on his tours. [18] Writing at the time when Congress was in special session to consider neutrality revision, Vanderbilt reported to the President that his heaviest opposition was in the farm districts. Father Coughlin was causing a lot of harm, and neither Herbert Hoover nor the President's son Elliott were helping the cause. [19] During October, in the Middle West Vanderbilt found growing opposition to changes in the Neutrality Law, and he wrote to the President that "there seems to be a strong feeling that you personally have sold out to Wall Street and the Munition Makers." He also expressed doubt about the President's ability at this time to win a third term. [20] Later in the month, in a confidential survey which Vanderbilt periodically submitted to the White House, he estimated that 51 per cent of the people in the section of the Middle West he had visited favored revision while 49 per cent were opposed. Like others, he wrote: "Recommendation: Putting into the field as fast as possible competent authorities to lecture, to be interviewed, to talk over the radio of the vital need to the world for Revision." [21]

The President's position in the fight to modify existing neutrality legislation must be appreciated in the context of the times. What were the external developments which served as the background for the bitter revision debate on the floor of the Congress in July, 1939?

Hitler had occupied Austria in March, 1938. The Munich agreement concerning the Sudetenland had been signed on September 30, 1938. On March 11, 1939, the Germans occupied Czechoslovakia, and on March 22 they seized Memel. France and Great Britain pledged themselves to defend Poland on March 31; on April 7, Italy occupied Albania. On April 28, Germany denounced the 1935 naval agreement with Britain and a ten-year non-aggression treaty with Poland and made new demands on that country. Summer came, and the battle for neutrality revision was in full swing. After having already defeated revision in the House of Representatives and approved postponement by a vote of 12 to 11 in the Senate Foreign Relations Committee, the Congress received the Presidential message on July 14. This was obviously a last ditch effort destined to fail; the administration was now asking the Senate to override its own committee.[22] Every effort was made to win support within the political arena. Leading members of both parties attended a special conference called by the President. It was on this occasion that Senator Borah made the often quoted remark, "I have my own sources of information which I have provided myself, and on several occasions I've found them more reliable than the State Department." On the floor of the Senate, Borah presented the opinion of many that there would be no war in Europe unless the United States encouraged the democracies to be aggressive.

By July 30, 1939, Congress decided that neutrality revision could wait. The public mood at this time seemed to be shifting constantly; it was torn between sympathy for Great Britain and France and the desire to stay out of the war at all cost. This indecision made itself felt in the Congress by a stalemate. As noted previously, the President for political reasons had adopted the strategy of remaining in the background in order not to alienate possible supporters of revision. Contemporary observers point to the politicians' deep distrust of the President. Roosevelt's strategy did not work, but whether "bold and precise executive leadership might have won over many wavering congressmen and stimulated a public ground swell in behalf of the arms-embargo repeal" is difficult to determine.[23]

The battle for neutrality revision was not won until November 4, 1939, when the President signed the new Neutrality Act of 1939. Compromises were made to achieve this final goal, and the "cash and carry" concept was one. The battle for revision in a special session of Congress is well-known, and no effort is made here to give a full report. The isolationists massed their total strength and put up a stubborn fight. Matching an all-out drive by the isolationists which included major addresses to the American people by Charles A. Lindberg,[24] Herbert Hoover, and a whole roster of Senators, the President made strenuous efforts to counter the highly successful propaganda of the isolationists.[25] Again the President limited his appeals, but he did attempt to win bipartisan support from the Congressional leaders. In this struggle the administration had the backing of some prominent business leaders. The President also called in two well-known Republicans, Alfred M. Landon and Frank Knox.

In another effort to halt the isolationists the President asked Clark Eichelberger to organize the public fight for revision. At the latter's suggestion, William Allen White, the widely known Republican editor of the *Emporia Gazette,* was summoned to head a group called Non-Partisan Committee for Peace through Revision of the Neutrality Act. With an eye on Catholic opposition to revision, the President personally sought the cooperation of Cardinal Mundelein and Bishop Sheil.[26] On an organized basis all the isolationists' statements and speeches were rebutted, and once the campaign to repel the isolationists' charges had been embarked on, a majority for the repeal of the arms embargo was attained. The support for repeal, differing from one region to another, never fell below 56 per cent.

CHAPTER IV

THE SHADOW LENGTHENS

On December 14, 1939, a few weeks after the climactic developments following Germany's offensive against Poland, President Roosevelt wrote a long letter to William Allen White. The outlook for the
future was glum, Roosevelt felt; and he was particularly perturbed by
the public's insensitivity to a dangerous situation. Speculating about
the possible consequences of a Rusian-German arrangement, the
President wrote:

"What worries me, especially, is that public opinion over here is
patting itself on the back every morning and thanking God for the
Atlantic Ocean (and the Pacific Ocean). We greatly underestimate the
serious implications to our own future and I fear most people are
merely going around saying:

" 'Thank God for Roosevelt and Hull — no matter what happens they
will keep us out of war. We have enormous confidence in their ability
to handle our international relations.'

"The Lord and you know perfectly well that Roosevelt and Hull
fully expect to keep us out of war—but, on the other hand, we are
not going around thanking God for allowing us physical safety within
our continental limits.

"Things move with such terrific speed, these days, that it really is
essential to think in broader terms and, in effect to warn the American
people that they, too, should think of possible ultimate results in
Europe and the Far East.

"Therefore, my sage old friend, my problem is to get the American
people to think of conceivable consequences without scaring the
American people into thinking that they are going to be dragged into
this war." [1]

Roosevelt never resolved this problem satisfactorily. He, more than
anyone else in the nation, saw clearly the meaning of the developments abroad, and appreciated the grave threat confronting the
United States. He tried to do the things that had to be done, but
he never managed to win full-hearted public support. He could not
gain this support without being absolutely frank with the people, yet
in his judgment more frankness would have increased the difficulty of
furnishing aid to the Allies. In Divine's estimation, in the six weeks
during which the administration struggled to get the Neutrality Law

revised in the special session, "the administration carried on the elaborate pretense that the sale of arms to the Allies was but the accidental by-product of a program designed solely to keep the United States clear of war." [2]

This same theme was subtly present in the President's fireside chat on the European war, delivered on September 3, 1939. In this address Roosevelt stressed the relationship between the fate of Europe and of America: "It is easy for you and for me to shrug our shoulders and to say that conflicts taking place thousands of miles from the continental United States, and, indeed, thousands of miles from the whole American Hemisphere, do not seriously affect the Americas — and that all the United States has to do is to ignore them and go about its own business. Passionately though we may desire detachment, we are forced to realize that every word that comes through the air, every ship that sails the sea, every battle that is fought, does affect the American future."

Pointing out it was tragic that we have "to live in a world that is torn by wars on other continents," he emphasized that "it is our national duty to use every effort to keep them [wars] out of the Americas." He then made the most frequently quoted portion of this speech: "This nation will remain a neutral nation, but I cannot ask that every American remain neutral in thought as well. Even a neutral has a right to take account of facts. Even a neutral cannot be asked to close his mind or his conscience."

Between the invasion of Poland and the Nazi march into Belgium the war proceeded almost quietly; no special event greatly shocked the American people into a realization of the precariousness of their own position. So much greater, therefore, was the public alarm when on May 10, 1940, the Germans moved into Holland and Belgium.

At a news conference on April 18, 1940, attended by members of the American Society of Newspaper Editors, the President told his audience that he was depending on the press to bring all of the facts of the world crisis, as well as "the possibilities, the potentialities" of the world situation before the American public. Observing that during the past few weeks there seemed to be an increased desire "on the part of the American public, to think things through," Roosevelt referred to a report he had received from his wife (the President often obtained information on the public temper from Mrs. Roosevelt). "I can tell you . . . off the record . . . [that she] came back from a lecture trip of three weeks and she noticed, even in the past week, that people were beginning to say to themselves and in questions to her, in the last week of this trip, 'What is going to happen *if?* What is going to happen *if?*' Before this Denmark episode and the Norway episode, there weren't nearly as many questions by the public. 'What is going to happen *if?*' That is the first time that I have seen a more general willingness on the part of the American public to say, 'What is going to happen *if?*' " [3]

An interesting illustration of the role of public opinion involves the status of Greenland. Though we wished to make certain that the Germans would not occupy Greenland, the administration was reluctant to have either Great Britain or Canada be responsible for its protection; it claimed that Greenland fell under the Monroe Doctrine as a part of the Western Hemisphere. However, when specifically pressed by the Canadian government as to whether we were prepared to defend the island, we tried to escape a direct response by obfuscation. Failure to take a clear stand was based on the fear that the isolationists might accuse the administration of interventionism.[4] For this reason the President hesitated to answer questions regarding Greenland raised at his April 12th press conference.

A week later, however, Roosevelt admitted in effect that he had been stalling because he was more interested in the social aspects of the problem ("the 17,000 splendid Eskimos who are living in Greenland") than whether or not Greenland belonged in the Monroe Doctrine. Roosevelt then stated that he made a mistake in psychology and gave the following explanation. "Where I went wrong is this: I did not think the American people would support me if I said that Greenland belongs in the Monroe Doctrine. But the American people are way out ahead of me and I think I am right in saying that most of the American people today, as most of you sense, would O.K. it if their Government said tomorrow that Greenland is inside the Monroe Doctrine. They are ahead of their Government. Now, that is the actual fact." [5]

At the same conference a question indirectly summarized the basic dilemma confronting the majority of Americans, including the President. A reporter, referring to Roosevelt's comments about Greenland, said:

"I was very much interested in your statement about Greenland, especially as it applies to the public opinion in this country. I wondered if you have any opinion to express which would be of interest to us, if you agree with me that two beliefs we have today are, perhaps, contradictory? On the one hand, I believe that the majority of the American people are firmly sold on the idea that we should stay out of this conflict. On the other hand, I also believe that the majority of people — and I will confine that to my own section of the country — are convinced that we have a very definite stake in this conflict. Now, is it possible that we can overemphasize the first to the point where we will weaken our position with regard to the second and will not be prepared to take steps which would be very right in protecting our position in the latter?" [6]

This was, of course, the kind of query the President wanted to avoid. He did not answer directly because he either did not understand, or more likely because he did not wish to deal with the basic issue raised. Roosevelt's evasiveness in this connection is in itself an interesting comment on his attitude at the time. He was not yet prepared to cast off the mantle of hesitation to provide more vigorous leadership.

It should be noted that Roosevelt would not agree with this interpretation of his role. He pictured himself as a sort of "John the Baptist — voice in the wilderness" as he continued to issue general statements about the Nazi menace.

"We have to look ahead to certain possibilities," he declared on May 23rd. "If I had said this out loud in a fireside talk, again people would have said that I was perfectly crazy: The domination of Europe, as we all know, by Naziism — including also the domination of France and England — takes what might be called the buffer out of what has existed all these years between those new schools of government and the United States. If those two are removed, there is nothing between the Americas and those new forces in Europe. And so we have to think in terms of the Americas more and more and infinitely faster." [7]

In other words, the President was saying that this interpretation of events was so unacceptable that he dared not suggest it for political reasons.

It is extremely difficult to document Roosevelt's attitude on the relationship between public opinion and leadership and his views on the role of the individual in a democracy. A quotation from a letter he wrote to Carl Sandburg is pertinent in this regard: "It is amazing that the independent voters of America — an increasing number of them — many of them without real education — do have that final ability to decide our fate and the country's fate 'in the deep silence of their own minds.'" [8] Here is a strong expression of faith in the political responsibility of the free individual.

Mrs. Roosevelt, at a conference she had arranged for the President with representatives of the American Youth Congress on June 5th, probably expressed with greater exactness and more eloquence the President's views on the connection between leadership and public opinion. At this conference Mrs. Roosevelt and Harry Hopkins remained behind after the President had excused himself. Referring to the discussion that preceded the Chief Executive's departure, Mrs. Roosevelt commented:

"I would like to say one thing which I sense from this meeting tonight is not really in the minds of most of the people here, and that is that anything that you want to get done in a democracy has got to be wanted by the majority of the people and, if you believe in democracy, you have got to work for the majority and have got to be willing to wait for it.

"I have done organization work practically all my life and I know that until you organize a thing down to the precincts and get a real demand from there up, there is not that majority demand for the thing and you cannot get it.

"You come away from this with the feeling that the President is willing to lead, but never too far in advance of public opinion, because that is the way things work in a democracy as understood by a politician and a democrat." [9]

While these remarks were undoubtedly made with economic and social issues in mind, they also shed light on the President's approach to the problem of isolationism.

In view of Roosevelt's general attitude – i.e., his sympathies for the democracies and his appreciation of the dangers of the Nazi onslaught – only his wife's observations help to explain his very mild and restrained annual message to the Congress on January 3rd. In part the President said:

"I can understand the feelings of those who warn the nation that they will never again consent to the sending of American youth to fight on the soil of Europe. But, as I remember, nobody has asked them to consent – for nobody expects such an undertaking.

"The overwhelming majority of our fellow citizens do not abandon in the slightest their hope and their expectation that the United States will not become involved in military participation in these wars.

"I can also understand the wishfulness of those who oversimplify the whole situation by repeating that all we have to do is mind our own business and keep the nation out of war. But there is a vast difference between keeping out of war and pretending that this war is none of our business.

"We do not have to go to war with other nations, but at least we can strive with other nations to encourage the kind of peace that will lighten the troubles of the world, and by so doing help our own nation as well."

While the President emphasized the close ties between a peaceful Europe and a prosperous America, the idea was presented in a manner which made it appear an afterthought. He was still catering to the isolationists, who at this time seemed to be in the majority. This was not meant to be a stirring message to awaken the American people to the dangers confronting their national security as well as that of other democracies.

At the previously mentioned youth conference on June 5th, Roosevelt made another interesting comment. A questioner, upbraiding the President for the fact that social legislation seemed to have taken a back seat to the needs of national defense, asked him why he had not carried "the fight to the people." From the public, the spokesman claimed, the President could have secured the support which would have pushed desired bills through Congress. In response to this challenge the President first referred to Lincoln, who "had to compromise to gain a little something." Then taking up a point introduced by Mrs. Roosevelt, who had emphasized the importance of Congressional impression of public opinion, the President added, "So often the individual Congressman or Senator is way behind the people and the people have got the responsibility of bringing him up to date. . . ." [10]

Possibly Roosevelt foresaw a series of events which might be sufficiently shocking and dramatic to arouse a public call for action. If this situation occurred, the stirring popular conscience could no longer be ignored by Congress. The thesis overlooked the problematic influence of time. The time factor is fundamental in foreign affairs. At the end of 1940, for example, the relationship between time, public opinion, leadership, and the dire position of Britain was crucial. And, in the final analysis, it was not the United States that saved Great Britain from invasion, but Hitler's decision not to invade. Only the attack on Pearl Harbor ultimately united the American people in the face of adversity.

Dependence upon the innate good sense of the people to make realistic and courageous decisions without strong leadership necessarily has inherent dangers. Particularly during the thirties there was in some of the western democracies a leadership which was not capable of facing political reality or of thinking courageously. The attempts made to explain and understand this "leadership" have not been entirely successful. [11]

A short excerpt from a letter written by James W. Gerard, a man with life-long experience in democratic party politics, a practicing lawyer, and an ambassador to Germany before World War I, provides a poignant insight. "Much as our sympathies may be engaged," he wrote to Senator Pittman on January 18th, "our interest is not in waging war, not in how the warring nations, changing sides fifty times in the last centuries, divide their real estate; but we do have an interest in the establishment of a just, stable and honorable peace. We have an interest in the rehabilitation of a torn and ruined world, in the reestablishment of trade and commerce and the friendly intercourse of nations." [12] This seems to reflect a typical sentiment of the time. Americans are sympathetic. They wonder how the European countries managed to get themselves into such a mess, but they want to dissassociate themselves from this troublesome situation. When the fighting is over, however, Gerard generously concedes we have an obligation to lend a helping hand to build a "just, stable, and honorable peace."

Chapter V

CABINET MEMBERS IN THE BREACH

During 1940 more and more spokesmen for the administration took to public platforms and the air waves to inform the American people about preparedness, and, in some instances, the issues of the European conflict. Secretary of the Navy Knox, along with Secretary of War Stimson, Secretary of Interior Harold L. Ickes, and several others, formed a special nucleus in the Cabinet that was constantly prodding the President to be more affirmative about supporting the Allies. Knox and Stimson, both well-known Republicans, were invited to join the Cabinet on June 19 in order to form a more representative body. The President initially approached Colonel Knox on December 10, 1939, not long after Knox had taken a forthright and firm stand against the Axis in his newspaper, the *Chicago Daily News.* "What has come over the traditional American spirit of courage and independence?" Knox asked on his editorial page on January 22, 1940. "From where do members of Congress derive the idea that it is popular to be afraid?" Adding another voice to those urging the President to be more outspoken about the necessity of aiding the Allies, the editorial called for a "clear, courageous voice in Washington to rally the old-time American spirit."

On April 11th Knox's paper published an editorial which deplored the lack of moral protest in the country and reiterated the theme cited previously:

"Is it possible that we do not care?

"Have we become so abject in our posture toward the rest of the world that we dare not speak?

"Have we so far succumbed to peace-at-any-price dogma that we are afraid to tell the world just what we think of foul wrong done to peoples whose only crime was to believe in, and practice, liberty, rear their families in the fear of God. . . .

"What is this palsy of spirit that has come over us? Why do our public men, disregarding the multiple evidence that American sympathy is overwhelmingly with those who fight against such dictatorships as those of Hitler and Stalin, seek after the applause of the timid few who tremble before the ruthlessness of a bloody-handed tyrant, and would shush every utterance that told in simple words of American abhorrence of the Stalin-Hitler alliance, and its brutal inhumanity, injustice and rapine, practiced at the expense of those who cannot defend themselves?"

At the very time that Colonel Knox was supporting preparedness and assistance for the Allies, Secretary Ickes recorded the following thoughts in his diary: "My own belief is that the Administration, and this particularly means the President, is at a definite crossroads. In time of war, or threatened war, the people want a strong man who will give them affirmative action. The British Empire is very likely to pay the final penalty for Chamberlain's Munich policy." [1]

With the dramatic advances of the German forces through Holland and Belgium, the American people were now for the first time concerned about the need to shore up their own defenses and there was strong public support with regard to this issue. Nevertheless, the leadership was not without its problems. Even Colonel Knox, a leading supporter of the Allied cause and an astute critic of the administration, did not appreciate the importance of building up the Army to the same extent as the Air Force and Navy. In a speech delivered on April 13th, he said: "After our experience in the last world war, it is simply unthinkable that we will ever again send overseas a great expeditionary force of armed men. Consequently all grandiose plans for a whole nation making war, with millions of soldiers in the field and other millions engaged in production of arms and supplies for these great armies, can be dismissed as unnecessary for our defense." [2]

Through the spring of 1940, Frank Knox continued to utilize the editorial page of the *Chicago Daily News* to express his sympathy for the Allies. An article of May 21st, entitled "The Hour of Decision," was one of the first clear calls for aid to our friends overseas. In it Knox adopted a much stronger tone than the President at this particular time, although Roosevelt had stressed in a message to Congress and in a fireside chat in May that we could only be secure if we did our best to assist the beleaguered nations of Europe. "It would be a wicked form of self-delusion," the editorial warned, "to affect to believe that the Allies are sure to win in the long run, and that we can, therefore, pursue our own affairs in peace, and let Europe take care of itself." Knox also called for the full economic and moral mobilization of the United States, so that we would be in a position to help the countries of Western Europe. Quoting the "kindly, peace-loving sage of Emporia," William Allen White, Knox added: "This is not time for leaders to consider party or factional advantage. All men and creeds and clans may well call upon our President to confer with leaders of all parties looking to a foreign policy providing for an increase in armaments to defend ourselves and for every economic effort to help the Allies."

After his appointment as Secretary of the Navy, Knox continued to issue clarion calls in the same robust style that characterized the *Chicago Daily News* editorials. On August 4th he stated: "There are still those who deny that we face an emergency at all. They say that the wars of Europe will not engulf us — if we only mind our own business. They say that no dictator, however mad, would dare attack the United States or any other part of the Western Hemisphere. They contend that strict neutrality — and two oceans — are this country's true protection. I wish this were true. But the tragic record proves the opposition. What the dictators want, they take."

While these were also the sentiments of the President, the latter still hesitated to speak out with equal frankness. With even more candor and "in the lion's den" Secretary Knox delivered the following cold, hard words of warning to the American Legion on November 11th: "We shall want to avoid war, but you do not avoid war in a world organized as this one is by being afraid. That is the way to invite it."

Roosevelt must be given considerable credit for naming both Knox and Stimson to his Cabinet although some critics felt that the incumbent Secretary of War, Woodring, should have been replaced sooner. Both Stimson and Knox, on their appointment, called for policies to which even the President had not yet fully committed himself. For example, Colonel Stimson not only backed the compulsory draft but also suggested that American ports might be opened to the repair and service of British ships. Similar views stated openly and frequently by these men and others gradually set in motion a swelling tide of public support and sympathy for the Allied nations.

A small group of persons in close contact with Secretary of the Interior Harold L. Ickes was distinctly dissatisfied with the government's inadequate methods of alerting public opinion. Both Ickes and Lewis W. Douglas, a former Congressman and Director of the Budget with close ties to the President, expressed disappointment with Roosevelt's fireside chat of May 26th on national defense; [3] and by the following month Ickes and Archibald MacLeish were ready to urge that war be declared. "I would support a resolution right now declaring war against both Germany and Italy," Ickes stated in his diary on June 15th. "We could not send soldiers but we could send munitions and ships and airplanes and permit volunteers. We could provide food and credits, and, in the meantime, we would have a real purpose in preparing at the utmost speed."

By August 4th Ickes was genuinely perturbed about the fact that the administration was not doing enough to mobilize public confidence. "Meanwhile," he complained in his diary, ". . . we are not even taking the country into our confidence with a view to educating it as to what the immediate future may hold for us. I believe that as the result of the lack of aggressive leadership, the appeasement spirit is growing and it is growing particularly among the people who hold economic power. In this connection, when Archie MacLeish drove into Washington with me on Friday morning, he told me of a group of writers, radio people, and publicists who are eager to go out on a nationwide campaign of education. He asked me whether this should be done without waiting further for the Government itself to organize an agency of propaganda. I told him that my advice was to start immediately without waiting for anybody, that we had already lost too much valuable time."

In November Ickes returned to the argument he had repeatedly presented to the President on previous occasions. He felt that Roosevelt ought to frankly and openly try to win full public support for aid to Britain. Like Douglas, Ickes concluded that not enough was being done for England and that the President was not playing as effective a role as he might because he was overtired and too dependent on Harry Hopkins. And the latter could not be depended upon to stand up to the President. Ickes wrote on November 23: "Bill Douglas wants the President to go out right away and tell the people what is actually involved, calling upon them for the very great sacrifices which they will have to make and which they will be expected to make. He believes that the people will respond to such a call and so do I. He also believes that no one but the President can do this and in that I also agree." Eight days later Ickes added:

"I strongly urged the President to make a speech to the country over the air as soon as possible on the international situation. This was along the line of my talk with Bill Bullitt the preceding week. This is not the first time that I have urged this upon the President, but now, with the campaign behind us, I have a greater hope of a successful outcome. My thought is that if things should become as bad as they very well might, the people would be shocked at the situation in which they would inevitably find themselves. They ought to be aroused to the danger that the country is in, and their patriotism and willingness to sacrifice themselves should be stirred up. The President listened sympathetically and said that he might make such a speech about December 17, after his return."

Roosevelt finally went before the nation in a speech presenting his clearest public exposition of the crisis on December 29th. As long as Britain remained free, the President declared, the United States did not have to fear attack. While "some of our people like to believe that wars in Europe and Asia are of no concern to us," he emphasized that it was of the greatest importance that the aggressors in Europe and Asia be prevented from controlling the ocean lanes leading to our hemisphere. "If Great Britain goes down," he warned, "the Axis powers will control the continents of Europe, Asia, Africa, Australia, and the high seas — and they will be in a position to bring enormous military and naval resources against this hemisphere. It is no exaggeration to say that all of us, in all the Americas, would be living at the point of a gun — a gun loaded with explosive bullets, economic as well as military." The President referred to the fact that he had been urged by many to talk to the nation: "During the past week many people in all parts of the nation have told me what they wanted me to say tonight. Almost all of them expressed a courageous desire to hear the plain truth about the gravity of the situation."

In this address the President forcefully stated that the Germans were a threat to our very existence. He used harsh words about the appeasers in our ranks. "The experience of the past two years has proven beyond doubt that no nation can appease the Nazis. No man can tame a tiger into a kitten by stroking it. There can be no appeasement with ruthlessness. There can be no reasoning with an incendiary bomb. We know now that a nation can have peace with the Nazis only at the price of total surrender."

Roosevelt derided those advocating a negotiated settlement; a peace with a gang of outlaws "would be no peace at all." He said that the British and their Allies were fighting a war against an unholy alliance and that "Our own future security is greatly dependent on the outcome of that fight." He added that "Our ability to 'keep out of war' is going to be affected by that outcome." President Roosevelt assured his listeners, as on many previous occasions, that American troops would not be sent overseas; he affirmed once more that "our national policy is not directed toward war." Critics felt that this emphasis detracted from the need to stress preparedness and sacrifice. The thought that America might actively have to come to the assistance of the hard-pressed Allies was never publicly entertained. The President stated, however, that if we acquiesced in the Allies' defeat we would probably be the next victim. Referring to our productive capacity, Roosevelt with one short statement summed up dramatically what he wanted America's role to be: "We must be the great arsenal of democracy." Calling for a great national effort to increase defense production, he expressed the conviction that the Axis powers would not win the war.

Public opinion underwent a remarkable change during 1940. The American people were now more aware of the possible impact of German aggression on their security, and they were prepared to make every effort to help the democratic nations in Europe. As a result of this shift of opinion, the isolationist leaders changed their grounds of attack by insisting that we were weakening ourselves to a dangerous degree by sending armaments abroad and that such aid would involve us in war. In his latest fireside chat the President had tried to meet the challenge, but his address still fell somewhat short of the expectations of those who felt he should be more forthright with the American people.

Examination of most of Roosevelt's 1940 speeches regarding America's role in the world would lead to the conclusion that the President never really attempted to grapple with future alternatives in realistic terms.[4] Given the sentiments and the considerable confusion, as well as a deeply inbred desire for peace at all cost, the most memorable presidential comments were invariably those in which he insisted we would attempt to mind our own business and virtually assured the nation we would stay out of the war. It is particularly noteworthy that even in the five important campaign speeches during the fall of 1940 the President said practically nothing which might awaken the country to the external danger. When mentioning foreign affairs, the emphasis was on the steadfast American policy of keeping the peace. Since the sentiment against intervention was still predominant, it is understandable that Roosevelt would say nothing to arouse the opposition which at the slightest suggestion of our possible danger immediately accused the President of actively trying to promote war. In a campaign speech in Cleveland on November 2nd, Roosevelt summarized very succinctly all the points he usually raised when he addressed himself to world affairs:

"There is nothing secret about our foreign policy. It is not a secret from the American people — and it is not a secret from any Government anywhere in the world. I have stated it many times before, not only in words but in action. Let me restate it like this:

"The first purpose of our foreign policy is to keep our country out of war. At the same time, we seek to keep foreign conceptions of Government out of the United States.

"That is why we make ourselves strong; that is why we muster all the reserves of our national strength.

"The second purpose of this policy is to keep war as far away as possible from the shores of the entire Western Hemisphere. Our policy is to promote such friendly relations with the Latin-American Republics and with Canada, that the great powers of Europe and Asia will know that they cannot divide the peoples of this hemisphere one from another. . . .

"Finally, our policy is to give all possible material aid to the nations which still resist aggression, across the Atlantic and Pacific Oceans.

"And let me make it perfectly clear that we intend to commit none of the fatal errors of appeasement."

These statements were gross oversimplifications which made it difficult for the public to understand the real issues, and therefore, impeded winning popular support for concrete measures when the need arose.

It is fascinating to observe how the President's foreign policy analysis operated on two entirely different planes and styles — one for public consumption and the other to meet the pressing challenges of day-to-day and long-range decision-making. Only two days after delivering his December 29th speech on national security, he wrote a letter to Ambassador Francis B. Sayre in Manila which demonstrates a much more sophisticated understanding of our ties with Great Britain than he had expressed to the public. Roosevelt, we discover, saw the survival of Britain in all its broad, global strategic aspects requiring world-wide commitments on the part of the United States.

In a letter to the President, Ambassador Sayre had stressed the importance of not getting involved in a war with Japan, so that we could concentrate all our efforts on helping Britain. Roosevelt's response to this observation was carefully considered and very revealing. He emphasized that we did not wish to go to war with Japan or with anyone else in the following statement: "For practical purposes there is going on a world conflict, in which there are aligned on one side Japan, Germany, and Italy, and on the other side China, Great Britain and the United States. This country is not involved in the hostilities, but there is no doubt where we stand as regards the issues. Today, Japan and Germany and Italy are allies. Whatever any one of them gains or 'wins' is a gain for their side and, conversely, a loss for the other side." [5]

The President went onto point out that the British Isles and her Dominions and Dependencies were on the defensive around the world. He concurred with Sayre that "our strategy should be to render every assistance possible without ourselves entering the war," but he raised the question whether we would be "rendering every assistance possible to Great Britain were we to give our attention wholly and exclusively to the problems of the immediate defense of the British Isles and of Britain's control of the Atlantic?" In response to Sayre's warning that the Japanese might move southward, Roosevelt observed that a Japanese move involving the Netherlands, East Indies, and the Malay Peninsula would improve German chances of victory. Roosevelt felt very strongly that the British had been able to protect themselves not only "because they have prepared strong local defenses but also because as the heart and the nerve center of the British Empire they have been able to draw upon vast resources for their sustenance and to bring into operation against their enemies economic, military and naval pressures on a world-wide scale."

Since, in the President's view, the world-wide ties and responsibilities were a source of strength to Britain, American assistance should not be restricted to the European theater. Because British defense strategy had to be global, Roosevelt felt that "our strategy of giving them assistance toward ensuring our own security must envisage both sending supplies to England and helping to prevent a closing of channels of communication to and from various parts of the world, so that other important sources of supply and other theaters of action will not be denied to the British." Roosevelt emphasized that while we had no intention of being "sucked into" a war with Germany, we would nevertheless do all we could to assist the Allies. [6] These views again show a recognition of realities which the President did not disclose in his more public comments. They were views with which his close associates, however, were familiar; and for this reason we may presume they were much disturbed when the President was not as open and frank as he might have been in his public statements. It is only in this context that we can appreciate Stimson's judgment that "no statesman in the world saw and described the Nazi menace more truly than Franklin Roosevelt." [7]

In the President's mind the hostilities on the different continents were all parts of a single world conflict. This is confirmed by a letter to Joseph C. Grew, our Ambassador to Japan, in which he wrote:

"Our strategy of self-defense must be a global strategy which takes account of every front and takes advantage of every opportunity to contribute to our total security."[8] Roosevelt pointed out that since our problem was one of defense, our policies must remain flexible so that we could "decide when and where and how we can most effectively marshal and make use of our resources."[9] There is no evidence that such a strategy was ever mentioned publicly.

We should examine the views of one other important member of the Cabinet, Secretary of War Henry L. Stimson. Along with Knox and Ickes, Stimson thought that the President was not doing all he might to alert public opinion, but Stimson became more critical of the President's policy at a later date than Ickes and Knox. When Stimson became Secretary of War he did not believe that war was inevitable, but by the end of 1940 he had changed his mind; and on December 16, 1940, he recorded in his diary "that this emergency could hardly be passed over without this country being drawn into the war eventually."[10]

Bundy reports that prior to the passage of the Lend-Lease Act Stimson felt that the President was moving as fast as the country wanted to go, and for this reason he did not criticize Roosevelt's national security speech on December 29th. But after approval of this Act by the Congress it was Stimson's "strong belief that the situation required more energetic and explicit leadership than President Roosevelt considered wise."[11] While the President was devising brilliant stop-gap measures to assist the Allies, he dared not submit these measures for public approval. Approval could only be won, he feared, after a damaging political struggle which, instead of promoting unity, would engender increased bitterness, thereby making positive action more difficult. For example, in 1940 Roosevelt was reluctant to test whether or not Congress would support repeal of certain provisions of the neutrality law. Instead he conceived the idea of Lend-Lease. The administration by a vote of 336-55 in the House of Representatives and 67-9 in the Senate received the requested appropriations for this program. The strong support indicates that the opposition was not as influential as the President had believed.

Another attempt to circumvent the judgment of public opinion concerns the demand for convoys. Convoys were essential, but Stimson reported in his diary on April 10, that the President had concluded that Congress would defeat such a request. Stimson commented, "On this point I am rather inclined to differ with him, provided that he took the lead vigorously and showed the reasons for it. Nevertheless, he had made a decision and it was an honest one." [12] Roosevelt finally announced the inauguration of a half-way measure referred to as a patrol system, which proved in practice not to offer adequate protection. On this particular occasion Stimson was especially disappointed with the President's failure, for Bundy has written that Stimson's whole concept of the duty of the Chief Executive centered on his obligation to act as the leader, and not merely the representative of public opinion. In this vein Stimson wrote in his diary on April 22, 1941, "I cautioned him [the President] on the necessity of his taking the lead and that without a lead on his part it was useless to expect the people would voluntarily take the initiative in letting him know whether or not they would follow him if he did take the lead." [13]

Stimson always had the highest respect for Roosevelt's political judgment, and he never stated that his method was wrong; he felt, however, that in the President's position he would have acted differently. In his opinion "the President would have been even greater a politician if he had been a less artful one."

Stimson had a heart-to-heart talk with Roosevelt in April and told him that the state of American public opinion toward the war had become less and less favourable. In connection with this conversation Stimson, according to Bundy, observed "that if the President were himself to go to the country and say frankly that force was needed and he wanted the country's approval in using it, he would be supported." Stimson's restlessness and good-humored dissatisfaction with what he felt were the shortcomings of the President's program are displayed in the following exchange reported by Bundy. "One day at a Cabinet meeting, 'the President talked a little about his program of patrol and what he was planning to do, . . . and after narrating what had been done he said, "Well, it's a step forward." I at once said to him "well, I hope you will keep on walking, Mr. President. Keep on walking." The whole Cabinet burst into a roar of laughter which was joined in by the President.' " [14]

Interestingly enough, Roosevelt did not object to strong speeches by members of his administration in support of an all-out effort to aid the Allies. Stimson, in a radio address approved by the President and delivered on May 6, came out for "active naval assistance for the British," offering the ominous warning that "unless we on our side are ready to sacrifice and, if need be, die for the conviction that the freedom of America must be saved, it will not be saved."

The President in the final analysis followed his own counsel, but he was not remiss in accepting recommendations for his speeches. Cabinet members, including Stimson, Knox, Ickes, and Patterson, were urging Roosevelt, particularly during the spring of 1941, to take a more vigorous approach with the public in explaining how the United States could best fulfill its obligations to the Allies. The State Department, however, usually acted as a restraining influence.

In a radio address on May 27, 1941, the President declared an unlimited national emergency, and announced that United States ships would patrol North and South Atlantic waters. In a subsequent press conference, however, much to Stimson's dismay Roosevelt indicated that this did not mean he would support the use of convoys. On May 24, Stimson had already gone so far as to suggest to the President that he request authorization from the Congress "to use naval, air, and military forces of the United States" to protect the lifeline across the Atlantic.

While Stimson felt that the Chief Executive had succeeded in alerting the American people to the Fascist danger, he had never stated clearly the ultimate consequences of the existence of this danger. Bundy observes that "to Stimson it always seemed that the President directed his arguments altogether too much toward his vocal but small isolationist opposition, and not toward the people as a whole." While Stimson would have admitted that "there are always times in politics when it is impossible to speak with entire frankness about the future," Bundy observes that "the essential difference between Stimson and the President was in the value they set on candor as a political weapon." [15]

At the end of May, Stimson forwarded an almost impassioned appeal for leadership to the President:

"From what has come to me on all sides I feel certain that the people of the United States are looking to you then to lead and guide them in a situation in which they are now confused but anxious to follow you. Under these circumstances I think it would be disastrous for you to disappoint them. They are not looking for a statement of expedients or halfway measures but for an elucidation of fundamental principles in a grave crisis and, as far as possible, for light on the path which we as a nation must tread to solve that problem.

"The whole world is divided into two camps separated by fundamental principles and methods. You are the leader of one camp. The American people should not be asked to make the momentous decision of opposing forcefully the actions of the evil leaders of the other half of the world possibly because by some accident or mistake American ships or men have been fired upon by soldiers of the other camp. They must be brought to that momentous resolution by your leadership in explaining why any other course than such forceful resistance would be forever hopeless and abhorrent to every honored principle of American independence and democracy." [16]

While such measures as lend-lease, [17] the destroyer-base deal, and convoying were handled by the President with great political skill, the real issue of America's future role was always avoided because these measures were offered to the public as means to help to keep us out of the war. The support that the public gave the President on the measures he instituted was surely a sign that the public was ready to heed presidential leadership; but the President continued to be governed in his decisions by the small but vociferous and well-organized isolationist minority.

Stimson, perhaps more than any other critic of Roosevelt, appreciated the overpowering difficulties that confronted the President. An excellent illustration of this is Stimson's view that Roosevelt at times was not frank enough with the Congress. But observing the bitter scheming on the part of some important Congressmen in connection with the Draft Extension Act, which was passed by a majority of one vote in the House on August 12, 1941, he could appreciate the President's lack of confidence in getting other important defense measures approved through the democratic process.

CHAPTER VI

A SAMPLING OF ELITE OPINION

It is impossible to estimate the extent to which the President was influenced by the correspondence he received from America's opinion elite. That he was interested in the correspondence from the general public is shown by his insistence on a careful tabulation of his mail and regular reports, to which he would at times refer in his press conferences. It is known, also, that the presidential staff was kept busy answering influential citizens, and anyone personally known to the President could expect a personal reply. There naturally was a close relationship between volume of incoming correspondence and development of a crisis. At the height of the Battle for Britain, for instance, the President's office was flooded with mail. Among the many telegrams received was one from President James Bryant Conant of Harvard University, urging Roosevelt to release as many airplanes as possible to the Allies.

General Watson, Secretary to the President, prepared the reply to this telegram, but it was signed by the President himself. General Watson stated that the President had been thinking along the same lines as Conant for several months and added, "I am very glad to have your reaction." [1] The same day the President also heard from Lewis W. Douglas, who also advocated aid to the Allies. This letter, like many others, informed the President about the attitude of the public from the vantage point of the writer, and it urged leadership. "Quite a segment of opinion favors immediate assistance to the Allies. A very large segment of opinion is rapidly drifting in this direction. A small segment is jelled in the mold of isolationism. A clear, ringing, forthright statement of the issue that is being decided in Europe, of the consequences to us if the Allies lose, and of the need to give them help during this critical period would, I think, crystallize that body of opinion which instinctively is not isolationist, and would enlist, if not overwhelming support, at least astonishing support."

The President's reply was informal but very informative. He began his letter: "Dear Lew: I beat you to it! Very many planes are actually on the way to the allies, deliveries to this Government being put off." He went on to explain that the best way to aid American defense was to make material available which might be used against the Germans. The paragraph quoted below is of special interest because it offers a rare insight into Roosevelt's thoughts and motivations, relating his course of action to his view of the public.

"So you see I am doing everything possible—though I am not talking very much about it because a certain element of the Press, like the Scripps-Howard papers, would undoubtedly pervert it, attack it and confuse the public mind. This is inadvisable even though I am personally well accustomed to it. I am glad you found the sentiment right in Arizona. Very soon there will be the simple statement you speak of." [2]

In an address at the University of Virginia on June 10, 1940, the President announced that military supplies would be made available to countries fighting the Axis powers.

During 1940 and much of 1941, Roosevelt continued to receive letters urging presidential leadership in the international situation. Most of the writers believed that the public was ready to support a policy of all-out assistance for the Allies if only the President could report and elucidate for the public what was happening in the rest of the world.

Again on December 16, 1940, Conant wrote expressing his concern "with the grave danger which this country now faces due to the possibility of a defeat of Great Britain by the Totalitarian Powers. . . ." Conant favored all-out aid to Britain without reservations. He expressed the following view on the importance of leadership:

"I am much disturbed at the lethargy which now seems prevalent in certain sections of the country, and the defeatist spirit in certain quarters which asserts that nothing that we can do can be of assistance in the critical months ahead.

"I am hoping that you will see fit to inform the American people by a series of talks of the grave implications of the present situation. You are the one person who can now give American opinion the orientation which appears to be necessary if the plans of those who are working to build up sentiment for a policy of appeasement are to be defeated. In such a series of talks you could show in a way that you alone are able to do just how the defeat of Great Britain or a compromise peace would jeopardize the future of free institutions in this country. Furthermore you could, of course, present the real facts in regard to the gravity of the situation. Lastly, you could point out effectively what assistance the United States could render immediately."

In his letter thanking Dr. Conant for his thoughtful message, the President wrote "I note your suggestion that I inform the American people concerning the grave implications of the present situation. I am glad to have that suggestion and think I shall make a radio address along the line you propose before the end of the year." [3]

With the elections behind him, Roosevelt could breathe more freely and make franker public statements. Just prior to the election he had won a courageous gamble on the public acceptance of the destroyer-base deal. In his press conference on November 8, 1940, without hesitation he announced that half our future war production would go to Great Britain.[4] He also broached the subject of lend-lease at a press conference on December 17th.[5] The President issued no broad policy statements stressing the existence of a national emergency, and he made no special appeals for national unity and sacrifice. Nevertheless, action was pursued quietly which permitted more effective assistance to the British. The administration effected reorganization of the rearmament program; Harry Hopkins was sent to England to promote further planning at the beginning of 1941; and after careful examination by the Congress, lend-lease was approved on March 11, 1941.

The American people remained emotionally confused, torn between sympathy for England and the stronger desire to remain free of involvement at all cost, buffeted between the extreme views of the isolationists, some favoring a negotiated peace, and a less vociferous group favoring intervention.[6]

Many who were sympathetic to the Allied cause continued to plead with the President to exert more leadership. On May 6, 1941, Hamilton Fish Armstrong, editor of *Foreign Affairs*, who occasionally corresponded with the President, sent him a lengthy analysis of the international situation that stressed the need for maximum American assistance for the British. The opinions he expressed are penetrating and shed much additional light on the leadership problem:

"I have watched with admiration in these last weeks the gradual development of your program of aid to Britain. I think I understand your ultimate objective and your cogent reasons for wishing to proceed step by step, leaving the final decisions to an overt act by the enemies of the United States or to the development of an even greater public demand here. But will our enemies commit an overt act? And will our people spontaneously rise to the emergency in time? I think the answer to both questions may possibly be 'No.' " [7]

Armstrong felt it quite possible that Hitler would avoid an overt act at all cost if American aid did not appear to be decisive in changing the odds then favoring a German victory; there would be no sense in forcing a showdown with the United States if Britain's defeat was almost assured.[8] He emphasized that, because of the danger of a collapse of morale in Great Britain, it was indispensable that "the British people should feel in their hearts and know in their minds that under your leadership we are already currently providing every possible iota of help regardless of the risks involved to us." How could we create the atmosphere that would permit giving maximum support to the British? Armstrong pointed out that: "On the basis of all the evidence available, your foreign policy has the support of a very substantial majority of the American people. But beyond this specific support for your announced aims your own character and person command an enormous popular admiration and respect. I believe that you can draw on this enormous fund at will." [9]

Armstrong argued that Hitler's timetable of aggression would not admit delay, that a major German strike at the British seemed imminent, and that the risks for the democracies could be reduced if we were committed to Britain's side before the attack came. Regarding public support for such a step, Armstrong wrote:

"You of course receive all sorts of reports about the public reaction to your foreign policy in different regions of the country. Isn't it true that, whatever these reports indicate there is little likelihood that the support for your policy as it has been developed up to this moment will ever be any greater than it is today? This is so not only because of the immense new activity now being undertaken by the America First groups, favored by the fact that they now have an announced and ambitious leader. It is also true because the various spokesmen on your side, numerous and energetic though they are, are handicapped by the fact that your policy of 'gradualness' cannot be explained to the public either in detail or as regards ultimate objectives, and hence that explanations and defenses of this policy necessarily remain vague, contradictory and ineffective." [10]

One of the most cogent memorandums received by the President was prepared on May 8, 1941, covering a conversation between Bishop Sheil, Chicago's liberal Catholic leader and R. J. Finnegan, editor of the *Chicago Daily Times.* The most pertinent part of the memorandum reported that the Bishop felt the people were groping in the dark. He expressed the wish that President Roosevelt would deliver "an all-out 'Fireside Chat' in which no holds are barred or punches pulled in taking the people of the Nation into your complete confidence. He feels that 'cracker barrel' days in forming public opinion are over, and that you are the only person who can effectively accomplish the need for our type of thinking. He states that he is not interested in any private information, but only information that the entire nation can and should have; and in this connection states that there is 'too much off-the-record talk in Washington; Washington needs more record talk.'

"He states that he has been sympathetic in part in permitting public sentiment to jell; but now is the time 'to move in' and give the people the truth, and that their response will electrify the national morale." [11]

Harold Ickes reports in his diary that Felix Frankfurter was also puzzled about the President's failure to mobilize public opinion. Ickes hoped that Frankfurter, who was close to Roosevelt, would broach this issue; but Frankfurter replied that outside influences should be employed. According to Ickes, Bill Douglas also felt that there was lack of leadership, and that something ought to be done to awaken the public. Ickes indicates, on the basis of information he had received, that the Chief Justice was alarmed about the state of public opinion and had declared his readiness to make a nationwide speech if the President personally asked him to.

On June 6, 1941, Roosevelt received a letter from James Warburg, the author and banker, which was similar in some respects to that from Hamilton Fish Armstrong. Mr. Warburg particularly analyzed the effects of the President's important radio address of May 27th, in which he declared an unlimited national emergency. The immediate effect of the broadcast, Warburg wrote, was that people felt relief in the sense that they now knew where they stood. Warburg added, however:

"Since the speech I have noticed both here and in Washington, from where I have just returned, a rapidly increasing spirit of depression and frustration among the very people who are your most loyal supporters, and I have noticed an increasing rise in the spirits of those who are working and hoping for a negotiated peace.

"The feeling among your supporters might be summarized like this:

"1. The British will to continue resistance is now based upon the absolute belief that we are coming into war with them. If this belief is shaken a collapse of British morale is almost certain. There is only a very short time left in which we shall either have to make their belief come true or face a breakdown of British resistance.

"2. It is the feeling among your supporters that you clearly realize this and unquestionably want us to take up arms before there is a collapse in Britain, but that you feel you have gone as far as you can go for the moment, that popular opinion has not yet caught up, that

in some form Congress must give you a vote of confidence, and that
Congress is not ready to do this — at least not without a protracted
and disastrous debate.

"3. That you are hoping that our enemies will provide us with an
incident which will take the decision out of your hands, but that this
is extremely unlikely because the Germans of 1941 are not the Germans of 1917. (Personally I am sure that you realize this better than
anyone else. I am merely reporting opinion as I have found it.)

"4. It is the feeling among your supporters that public opinion
is far more ready for action than you assume and that only action will
solidly unify the country.

"5. It is the feeling that inaction, even for a short time, may in a
military sense make it impossible to carry out the policy you enun-
ciated in your broadcast and may also rapidly strengthen the opposition here at home." [12]

In conclusion Warburg emphasized, that whatever action the President might take, it should be carried out as a *fait accompli*. Indirectly
this was certainly an admission on his part that Congress was in a
mood to delay, perhaps even to prevent, any administrative action.

It is difficult today to appreciate the heavy pressures to which the
President was then subjected. There were those who supported involvement to serve our security interests; others felt that America
should promote a negotiated peace or stay out of the European war.
The President's position seems clearer in retrospect than it might have
been at the time.

Pressed, as he often was, to make a strong speech, he once replied
according to Ickes: "I am not willing to fire the first shot." Ickes and
others believed, of course, that Hitler would not move until he was
ready, presumably after all European opposition had been eliminated.

On June 22, 1941, another dramatic factor was added to the already
complicated leadership problem. Churchill and Roosevelt had previously agreed they would support the Soviet Union if it were attacked
by Germany. During the Spring of 1941 British intelligence reports
predicted that this event would take place soon. After Russia was
attacked, the President made it clear that we would not invoke the
Neutrality Act, and a special supply committee was created to operate
under the supervision of the State Department. The immediate reaction of the general public seems to have been one of increasing justifi-
cation and support of more aid for Great Britain. The new partner in
the struggle against the Axis was readily accepted by the interven-

tionists, while the isolationists expressed the hope that the Germans and Russians might mutually exhaust each other.

We may conclude that Americans generally were on the side of the Russians, but this is a generalization that must be examined in more detail. National polls taken subsequent to the attack indicated that the "extreme isolationists" continued to preach complete separation from the struggle; the "middle of the road" interventionists, who rejected direct participation in the war, supported aid for Russia on the assumption that this would help America to stay out of the war. The sentiments expressed by the isolationists at this point could not be ignored, however. No immediate action was taken by the administration. Though the President offered to make aid available to the Soviet Union, no specific commitment was made at this time. Raymond H. Dawson observes that "the ideological issue was thus exploited to the fullest by isolationist spokesmen. They thrust it to the forefront in almost every instance and depicted the threat of communism as one more deadly than that faced in nazism." [13]

By the time lend-lease appropriations were approved in the House of Representatives on October 10, 1941, by a vote of 328 to 67, support for the exclusion of the Soviet Union from lend-lease had died to a whisper. In the Senate the appropriations bill was passed by a vote of 59 to 13, and the exclusion of Russia was never seriously considered. Studies indicate that by October there was strong editorial support for a policy of aid to Russia, and the public opinion polls showed support for a Russian aid program. On October 30th Stalin was informed by the Administration that one billion dollars of lend-lease aid would be made available. This action was taken in face of a small but still highly vocal opposition as represented by the *Chicago Tribune* and the *New York Journal-American.*

As for the issue of presidential leadership, particularly in the days immediately following the Nazi invasion of the Soviet Union, there was some feeling that Roosevelt could have acted more effectively in guiding public opinion. On July 1, 1941, William C. Bullitt wrote the President as follows:

"The emotions aroused by the spectacle of Nazis fighting Bolsheviks were so conflicting that most people needed a lot more guidance than they got. Public opinion is now befuddled. The feeling has begun to spread that we no longer need to hurry our war preparations and that the communists have become the friends of democracy.

"I think you should take the first opportunity — perhaps your next press conference — to point out:

"1. That the German attack on the Soviet Union makes it essential for us to produce with greater speed than ever, since Germany may soon have all the resources of the Soviet Union at her disposal." [14] Ickes wrote in his diary that it was fortunate that Winston Churchill had so quickly and forthrightly spoken in favor of lending support to Russia, particularly because "there was not a word from the President." Speculating that perhaps Roosevelt could not make up his mind on what the American attitude should be, Ickes said: "It would be just like him to wait for some expression of public opinion instead of giving direction to that public opinion." Rather cynically, Ickes added: "He [Churchill] steadied us, he gave us the right line, and our more slowly moving President caught up with him by Tuesday, when, at a press conference, he let it be known, without any eloquent outburst on the subject, that we would aid Russia under the Lend-Lease Act, as we are aiding Great Britain. Of course, as a matter of fact, we are not aiding Russia because we can't get supplies to her, so that what the President said indicated a state of mind rather than an active policy." [15]

In the final analysis, the question of aid to the Soviet Union was not an issue of primary importance in the Congressional approval of lend-lease because international developments, particularly with respect to the crisis on the high seas and increased tensions in the Far East, had led the isolationists to place their emphasis on staying out of the war.

Chapter VII

POISED AT THE BRINK

It is easier to demonstrate that public opinion is capable of exerting dramatic pressures on presidential decision-making than to delineate precisely the effects of this pressure on the formulation of presidential policy. In the documentation cited, one notices a remarkable dearth of specific evidence as to how the President evaluated the wishes of the citizenry. On the basis of Roosevelt's actions, we may conclude that public opinion played a significant role in determining the pace at which he set forth and pursued his policies. However, any conclusions regarding the President's views of public opinion are highly speculative and are based on a study of presidential policy rather than on any direct substantiation. Our study makes it clear that President Roosevelt had a fundamental interest in the manipulation of the sentiments of the electorate to serve the policy he considered vital for the promotion of national security. There are a number of statements which, I believe, shed additional light on his regard for public sentiment. An interesting comment on this, particularly because it is so rare, is to be found in a letter written by the President to Crown Prince Olav in Oslo. Expressing American sympathy for Scandinavia and the desire to help the northern countries which had been attacked, the President referred to the frustrating obstacles barring any assistance. The old bitterness regarding unpaid war debts to the United States is one barrier, he pointed out, despite the fact that the Scandinavian countries are not indebted to us. Finland, the one northern country that did owe, had paid her debt with regularity. With particular reference to the repeal of the arms embargo the President felt that delays must be explained by the fact that "most of the Members of Congress are thinking in terms of next Autumn's election." Looking at these delays philosophically the President added "that is one of the prices that we who live in democracies have to pay. It is, however, worth paying if all of us can avoid the type of government under which the unfortunate population of Germany and Russia must exist."[1]

Referring to the convoy issue, although the statement can be applied more generally, Langer and Gleason conclude that Roosevelt resorted to silence whenever he became "increasingly uncertain of his hold over public opinion"; and he became "correspondingly reluctant to risk his leadership." [2] He, therefore, genuinely appreciated the initiative shown by the Committee to Defend America by Aiding the Allies whose original success at gaining adherents for the idea of American aid to Britain was formidable. Mr. William Allen White, its mentor, played such a significant role that it was also referred to as the White Committee. The President's consciousness of White's work and the importance of the committee is indicated by his comment that he "was really disturbed when I heard you were leaving the Chairmanship." [3]

Replying to a letter written by Senator Bailey of North Carolina, Roosevelt clearly acknowledged that the administration must attempt to explain its policies by emphasizing the national interest. He touched on a letter that he had recently received from a nationally known advertising executive and agreed that the isolationists ("the Wheelers, Nyes, Lindberghs, etc.") were successful in their attack against the administration because they argued that our actions were intended "to save the British Empire, rather than ourselves." The President concurred that it is necessary to stress "that we are not concerned with the affairs of the British Empire but are concerned with our own safety, the security of our own trade, the future of our own crops, the integrity of our own continent, and the lives of our own children in the next generations. That, I think, is a pretty good line to take because it happens to be true and it is on that line itself that we must, for all the above purely selfish reasons, prevent at almost any hazard the Axis domination of the world." [4]

He wasted no time putting his own advice to good use. At a press conference held especially for editors of business publications on May 23, 1941, the President, referring to the Aid to Britain movement, stated that "a great deal of this perfectly well-intended publicity has been stupid." In a direct and simple manner he impressed his listeners with the idea that all our actions were carried out with our self-interest in mind.

"I begged them when they started the so-called Aid to Britain movement—I said, 'You know there are an awful lot of people in this country that don't personally "give a continental" about Aid to Britain, but on the other hand, if you tell the whole sentence you get people to understand.'

"What is the whole sentence? 'America First Through Aid to Britain.' Now that's a very different thing; that tells the truth. You are working for America first, because England today is holding the line and is doing practically all the fighting. Now the real sentence is, 'Let us keep America going by giving aid to Britain while we are arming ourselves,' and that is the thought to get across." [5]

Roosevelt urged his audience to eliminate prejudices aroused by inept slogans and reminded them that the President of the United States was the real leader of the America First movement.

The available evidence seems to demonstrate that Roosevelt was more "hawk" [6] than leader with respect to public opinion. Some Congressmen explained their opposition to the extension of the draft on the basis that the President had never made a clear statement on the danger. Though he talked with great skill in his press conferences about the effects of a Nazi victory, he was not quite as effective on this subject in his formal addresses. On March 20, 1941, Hadley Cantril wrote to Mrs. Anna M. Rosenberg, "When listening to the President's speech the other night I was then, as I have been so frequently, somewhat disappointed that he did not spell out any more specifically the personal effects of a Nazi victory or the whole Nazi ideology." [7]

Especially during 1941, nearly every major presidential talk was preceded by public demands for leadership and followed by criticism that the speech had fallen short of what the crisis demanded. We have already referred to the President's important radio address of May 27, 1941, in which he proclaimed the unlimited national emergency. But Stimson, Ickes, and others thought he had not sufficiently informed the American people. Prior to the speech but in reference to it, an editorial in the *Memphis Commercial Appeal* read: "Lay it on the line, Mr. President." The editorial expressed the hope that the President would be "candid and realistic." "Good arguments, reasonable arguments, logical arguments, can be developed on either side," the writer stated. "Division of opinion among the people is common and characteristic in this democracy," but, said the writer, it is not a question for debate that the nation is looking for national leadership. [8]

By far the most fascinating analysis of the "great agitation in the United States . . . over the President's leadership" is to be found in an article by Raymond Gram Swing for the *London Sunday Express* dated May 11, 1941. [9] Swing pointed out that the President was in a difficult position: on the one side were his closest friends who were impatient with his leadership and particularly with his reluctance to tell the nation the whole truth; on the other side were his opponents who "are ready to close in on him like wolves and rend him for hesitancy, inconsistent drifting and inability to lead."

Swing acknowledged that he has no firsthand knowledge of the

President's strategy for winning the necessary public support for American involvement on the Allied side. But he feels confident of the accuracy of his analysis because "President Roosevelt has a sense of history, of the nature of democracy, and of deep responsibility, so that the inside of his mind is hardly a secret."

What then was the basis, in Swing's view, for the President's reluctance to press for American intervention in the European war?

"It is incontrovertible to say that the entry of the United States in this war (and equally so, the refusal to enter it) is the most important decision that the country has had to make in its entire history. The war promises to be long, and the future to which it leads is as obscure as any ever faced by a nation. The war would inevitably reveal many defects in American efficiency. It would find us, like the other democracies, late in our preparations. The time would come when the public would rebel against glaring evidences of ineptness and unpreparedness. Its morale would be shaken, along with its faith in its leadership. Mr. Roosevelt knows this would lie ahead. If he should assume the leadership now and appear to be 'taking' the country into war, the public would turn on him later, and reproach him for having brought the country to its dark hours. At such times, the only possibility of maintaining unity and morale is that the President shall not have whipped up sentiment for the war, that he should appear to have yielded to public insistence, and that the war should be an enterprise of partnership, rather than something entered at his behest."

Swing felt that Roosevelt was very conscious of the difference between the presidential and the parliamentary system in a crisis situation. In the latter system, if leadership proves inadequate, a Chamberlain can be replaced by a Churchill. Under the presidential system, the leader must attempt to carry on the affairs of state even if his position has been undermined by his opponents and public criticism and other obstacles hamper his efforts at policy formulation. Swing emphasized Roosevelt's personal appreciation of his own limitations in the following words: "What is important, in its deepest historic meaning, is not American entrance into the war, but American effectiveness. And the shape of that contribution is being moulded now to some extent, and will be definitely moulded by the character of the entry. America must come in, if it comes, after full discussion, with a feeling of having known the facts, and having been allowed to make up its mind. That is the democratic way. It is the way which Roosevelt understands and values, not only as an ideal, but as the hardest kind of political realism. He cannot gamble with such precepts. The life and safety of the nation depend on his most scrupulous loyalty to them. He must choose a time for assuming leadership which makes for strength and reliability later on."

The impatience with Roosevelt's leadership which we have discussed in the foregoing pages "paradoxically becomes part of the Roosevelt strategy" Swing wrote. The more impatience that can be mustered, the sounder the position of the President: "The more his friends are in anguish about his inscrutable delay, the better they serve him. The more vocative the protests in newspapers and at public meetings, the safer the future, and the sounder the President's leadership when it comes. That is not to say that he is egging his associates on to create a demand, which is not an accurate way to describe the situation. He feels that the public is not yet aware enough of the dangers and the gravity of the hour for him to move now. That being his view, he still does not undertake to instruct the public himself. That is for others to do, and do with all eloquence and alacrity. They are doing it. Hull, Knox, Stimson, and Willkie,[10] the four most authentic secondary leaders in the country, are hammering and teaching."

Swing concluded that May 1941 was not yet the "occasion for the President to organize and educate, to cajole and to threaten." A decision to stand with the Allies must be an American decision to be worthwhile. It must first be a national decision "before it can be Roosevelt-led."

Swing gives a challenging account of the forces which motivated the President. It enables us to see his actions in a positive and constructive light. But this analysis presents Roosevelt as a better tactician than he really was, and it makes him a better statesman than even a great politician in a democracy can be. The political maneuvering during 1940 and 1941, as well as in previous years, indicated a desire to avoid direct confrontation with public opinion on the issue of America's role in world affairs. The record shows that, in the four years from the Quarantine address to the Pearl Harbor attack, the President made no further speeches to promote the idea of collective security. The standard explanations for Roosevelt's position are well-known: the administration could not afford a serious political defeat in the Congress on the issue of American interventionism, nor could the President afford to deepen the bitter divisions of opinion that were current in our country before the Second World War.

Studies of this period do not agree in their appraisal of Roosevelt's role. Selig Adler says that an evaluation of the President's leadership cannot be based on the historical evidence alone; it involves a value judgment concerning the effective strength of the isolationists if the United States had been drawn into a declared war in Western Europe without the attack on Pearl Harbor. Langer and Gleason conclude that an out-and-out proposal to declare war would certainly have been defeated even on the very threshold of the Pearl Harbor attack. Adler notes that the President would have had to contend with partisan dissent.[11] Another study finds that, without the attack on Pearl Harbor, "United States' entry into the war would have been postponed—possibly indefinitely."[12] These conclusions underestimate the support in the country for the concrete measures that had been taken by the President to aid the Allies, and particularly they evince a lack of appreciation of the leadership role of the President, whose potential had not yet been fully employed to alert the American people.

CHAPTER VIII

THE PRESIDENT EXPLAINS HIS ROLE

During his Presidency, Harry Truman rarely expressed his views on the role public opinion plays in determining policy, but we know from his speeches and writings that he gave considerable thought to the function of executive leadership in a democracy. In his book *Mr. Citizen* he states: "The most dangerous course a President can follow in time of crisis is to defer making decisions until they are forced on him and thereupon become inevitable decisions. Events then get out of hand and take control of the President, and he is compelled to overcome situations which he should have prevented. When a President finds himself in that position, he is no longer a leader but an improviser who is driven to action out of expediency or weakness." [1]

In other words, the reluctance of public opinion to support an administration on a particular issue should not prevent or restrain executive action. Lack of decision may be detrimental to the national security or welfare; the President cannot wait until he has the full support of the people on every decision he makes. "In normal times," Truman continued, "lack of Presidential leadership may be harmless, though it can hardly be considered a national asset." However, times were not normal during the Roosevelt and Truman administrations, a point Truman emphasized: "All the time I was President, one event followed another with such rapidity that I was never able to afford the time for prolonged contemplation. I had to make sure of the facts. I had to consult people. But to have hesitated when it was necessary to act might well have meant disaster in many instances." [2]

Rapid decisions were essential in the development of the Truman Doctrine, the Marshall Plan, our response to the Berlin blockade, and the outbreak of the Korean war.

Truman has frequently stated that the point of departure for all decisions must be a fundamental faith in democratic government and the desire to make decisions that will best further the welfare and the security of the people. But sometimes, as he has pointed out, one must recognize that there exists only "a choice of evils, in which case you try to take the course that is likely to bring the least harm."

Truman operated within a framework of a broad general principle which he would apply to specific problems. As he has said, quick decisions had to be made; and if you made a mistake, you would try to correct it as quickly as possible by making another decision. His views are concisely expressed in these words: "A President ought not to worry whether a decision he knows he has to make will prove to be popular. The question is not whether his actions are going to be popular at the time but whether what he does is right. And if it is right in the long run it will come out all right. The man who keeps his ear to the ground to find out what is popular will be in trouble." [3] This philosophy by itself would not be an acceptable formula for sound political leadership. Leadership is more than the ability to make the right decision and to oversee its execution; it is also the ability to mobilize public sympathy and to generate public confidence.

President Truman gathered the facts, consulted the experts, and then made the final decision according to his best judgment. He has often been quoted as saying that a good leader must be a good politician, and the second role requires by definition an interest in public opinion. A political leader must make his decisions as he sees them, but he has a further obligation to the public: "A politician must be in a sense a public-relations man. Most leaders have been such men. They have had the faculty of presenting the ideas for which they have stood in such a way that the people have understood them and had confidence in them. If they had not been able to make others see as they did, they would not have been leaders." [4]

President Truman recognized that the office of the President has a great reservoir of prestige which must be responsibly and skillfully utilized by the Chief Executive to win support for his policies; he recognized also that it was his obligation to get the facts before the people in every possible way.

At one point, while addressing a group of school administrators, Truman recommended an article by Clinton Rossiter in the *Yale Review* because he felt it gave a satisfactory "approach to what is expected of the President and what he has to do." [5] Today, students of government are familiar with Rossiter's analysis of the eight major functions of the modern President. Referring to one of these functions, Rossiter writes that the President is the Voice of the People. In explanation, Rossiter states that, while it is true that public opinion has become a potent social force, "The focal position of the President as formulator or expositor of the nation's opinion is obvious. What Professor Wilson wrote, President Wilson demonstrated, 'His is the only national voice in affairs.'" Quoting Wilson again, Rossiter says that the President must act as "the spokesman for the real sentiment and purpose of the country."⁶ President Truman evidently approved of this interpretation. He recognized the educative responsibility of his office when he affirmed: "I have always believed that the vast majority of people want to do what is right and that if the President is right and can get through to the public he can always persuade them."⁷ In judging the mood of public sentiment, he reported: "I made it my business as President to listen to people in all walks of life and in all fields of endeavor and experience."⁸ Of course, this is not necessarily the best way of gauging the pulse of public opinion. But Truman was convinced that public opinion polls do not represent a true cross section of American opinion, and he indicates in his *Memoirs* that he does not have a very high regard for people who allow themselves to be influenced by polls. In Truman's writings generally, the two subjects of public opinion and leadership are interrelated. Thus, his main thesis can be summarized as follows: effective leadership makes for an effective democracy. The following short passages emphasize this idea. The President wrote in his *Memoirs:* "I believe that the power of the President should be used in the interest of the people, and in order to do that the President must use whatever power the constitution does not expressly deny him." And in a speech delivered in 1954, he said "a successful administration is one of strong presidential leadership. Weak leadership — or no leadership — produces failure, often disaster."⁹

As a politician, President Truman appreciated the importance of public opinion; as a democrat, he expressed his faith in public opinion; but as a realist, particularly with respect to foreign policy, he believed that decisions must be taken without considering public opinion. These principles are not necessarily inconsistent.

Although Truman discussed the topic of public opinion infrequently, he made several interesting observations on the subject in 1949. First of all, he emphasized that "where the facts are available" the American people have a special obligation to inform themselves with regard to important international issues. Furthermore, our "foreign policy is not made by the decision of a few. It is the result of the democratic process and represents the collective judgment of the people. Our foreign policy is founded upon an enlightened public opinion." President Truman then presented a rather idealistic description of the role of public opinion: "The importance of public opinion in the United States is not always understood or properly evaluated. Public opinion in a country such as ours cannot be ignored or manipulated to suit the occasion. It cannot be stampeded. Its formation is necessarily a slow process, because the people must be given ample opportunity to discuss the issues and reach a reasoned conclusion. But once a democratic decision is made, it represents the collective will of the nation and can be depended upon to endure." [10]

The President cited examples to prove that the major foreign policy decisions since the war had been made "on the basis of an informed public opinion and overwhelming public support."

In another of his rare public comments on the role of public opinion Truman said at the University of Missouri:

"The democratic process is not always easy. It involved us in great public debates. Emotions are aroused and feelings run high.

"But when the shouting is ended and decision is taken, the resulting choice rests on the solid foundation of the common wisdom of the people.

"The ability of our democratic process to find proper solutions for difficult problems has been drastically demonstrated again in the last five years in the field of foreign policy." [11]

Truman added that we were the most powerful nation in the world at the end of the Second World War, and our leadership was needed to help other countries recover. This served our own interests. "The overwhelming choice of the American people" President Truman concluded, "was — and is — against the dangerous futility of isolationism and for full cooperation with other nations toward peace and freedom."

What if the choice of the American people had been otherwise? The President would argue, I believe, that some problems are too complicated and lie too close to the nation's vital interest to allow the American people to decide whether we would revert to isolationism by promoting the "Fortress America" concept or whether we would cooperate with other nations. These are decisions the Executive has to make himself. Once the decision is made, using the prestige of his office and exercising political leadership, the President must lead the campaign to win public support for a policy already delineated (i.e., collective security). Truman wrote in 1948, "I am hoping that we can educate the public to the foreign policy of the United States. . . ." He was the first to recognize that sooner or later the public must give its general consent to a program, if it is to be pursued successfully. Yet the public will have had little or no concern with the initiation of the new policy.

There is a remarkable identity of views between Harry Truman and Woodrow Wilson on the need for a strong executive in the field of foreign affairs. Wilson wrote in the preface of the fifteenth edition of his *Congressional Government,* "When foreign affairs play a prominent part in the politics of a nation, its Executive must of necessity be its guide: must utter every initial judgment, take every first step of action, supply the information upon which it is to act, suggest and in large measure control its conduct." [12]

Though Presidents Truman and Roosevelt did not have identical views on the utility of public opinion polls, they agreed that informal contacts with people could sometimes elicit useful information. President Truman wrote in this regard: "I made it my business as President to listen to people in all walks of life and in all fields of endeavor and experience. I did not see only the people who ought to be seen — that is, those who were 'well connected.' I always tried to be a good listener. But since the responsibility for making decisions had to be mine, I always reserved judgment." [13]

Both Presidents appreciated the importance of the press in disseminating the information which hopefully would generate public support for policy decisions. President Truman was succeeding a reputed master in this use of the most important information media. On balance, however, he himself handled the press conference as successfully as his predecessor, and was certainly much less critical of the press corps than President Roosevelt. It is true that, as the international tensions mounted, President Roosevelt was increasingly on edge with the press because of the position of the editorialists (and they were bitterly attacked by the President). [14] President Truman, however, saw each press conference as an effective instrument for the purpose of educating and molding American public opinion.

Both Presidents were quite persuasive in smaller meetings with more specialized groups. This form of "off-the-record exposition" was employed by President Truman particularly with regard to the single issue that most concerned the administration during his first term — the winning of public support for its foreign aid policy. Six special off-the-record press conferences were planned for the purpose of explaining foreign aid to various professional groups. [15]

The record indicates one very important difference between Presidents Roosevelt and Truman in their attitude toward the press, succinctly summarized by Bert Andrews of the *New York Herald Tribune.*

"President Truman's belief that the reporters have been eminently fair in covering his conferences is in contrast with the opinion frequently voiced by Mr. Roosevelt who often denounced the press in general. Sometimes he criticized publishers and columnists, while exempting the reporters confronting him. At other times he teed off on some of the reporters, too.

"President Truman has described his own outlook in the matter often enough to explain part of the difference between his view and that of Mr. Roosevelt. President Truman believes that as long as he gets objective treatment in the news columns he is being treated fairly. He concedes that it is the job and prerogative of editorial writers and columnists to express their own opinion, whether it is favorable or unfavorable to the President." [16]

It is interesting to observe the number of occasions on which Truman praised the press for its fair presentation of the facts, particularly with regard to such controversial matters as aid to Greece and Turkey and the Marshall Plan. In one press conference he told newsmen he was very pleased that aid to Greece and Turkey had been placed before the country in a way that the people could understand.[17] Less than a month later he expressed similar sentiments, adding "I think the press made a great contribution toward informing the people of the United States — toward showing just exactly what the intention of the legislation is." [18] A few weeks afterward he told a group of broadcasters that "what we need principally is to get an ethical viewpoint for purveying the news. I don't care what a fellow says about me on the editorial page, if you give me a fair break in the news." [19] Addressing a group of radio news editors in November, President Truman acknowledged the relationship between the mass media and its very powerful effect on public opinion.[20] He strongly believed that when the public was presented with the facts, it was ready to support executive initiative.

CHAPTER IX

THE PUBLIC'S VIEW OF THE SOVIET UNION

The ability of the United States to restrain expanding Soviet influence at the end of the Second World War depended primarily upon the maintenance of our military strength and upon a demontion of the willingness to utilize our influence to achieve an equitable balance of power in central Europe and in Asia. Although the United States in the immediate postwar period had decided to follow a policy of firmness, the administration, under the leadership of the President, had to make a conscientious effort to get the facts before the public and to explain the intricacies of certain situations as they developed.

Although we gradually came to realize that whenever we acted strongly "the Soviets backed away," the immediate postwar period did not lend itself to a rigid policy. Our concern at the end of the war was not with territorial settlements. All our hopes for peace lay in an international organization founded on Big Three membership and unity. Rostow makes the following observation: "This overriding American interest in the creation of conditions for world peace — rather than with the details of territorial power — accurately reflected both old American patterns of thought and a fatalistic conviction that American forces could not be kept in Eurasia beyond a few post-war years. Thus the nation did not define or seek systematically to achieve the power position requisite for the achievement of the grand design." [1]

Even if the United States had made all the proper military and diplomatic moves and had been able to win public support for what might have been a policy of brinksmanship, as Rostow points out, this still was no guarantee that we could have shaped the world to our liking.

Immediately after the war we were in an ambiguous position because on the one hand we were demobilizing rapidly, and on the other hand we feared an end to Big Three unity if the Soviet Union were antagonized. The public was convinced that a showdown with the Soviet Union would be self-defeating. For this reason, Rostow says that if America had wanted to take the initiative to salvage any part of the Yalta and Potsdam agreements, the government would have had "to prepare the public for a general showdown with Stalin. . . ." [2]

An apt illustration of this dilemma may be seen in a memorandum written by the American Ambassador to Poland. Ambassador Lane's comments represent a point of view that was increasingly appreciated in Washington. He wrote as follows:

"All of this, of course, boils down in the last analysis to a decision as to what our policy is going to be towards the Soviet Union. My own feeling is that unless we give publicity to what is going on in Poland and other nations in an analogous position, we will not be able to use our influence in these countries either politically or economically. With the withdrawal of the greater part of our armed forces from Europe we have lost one of the few arguments which are effective with a power such as the Soviet Union. In answer to the criticism which would undoubtedly be made that we are courting war with the Soviet Union in making the unpleasant facts known regarding Communist domination of the countries of Eastern Europe, ... I should like to say that the American public has a right to know the truth; that unpreparedness nearly cost us the last war, due to the isolationist attitude of a part of the people of the United States; that appeasement will be just as dangerous today as it was at the time of Munich; and that we run much more danger of war if we ignore the dangers of aggression than by honestly facing the facts." [3]

It has been suggested that in the months immediately after the war no one "could have summoned the strength to imagine the implications of what was happening in Lublin and Bucharest." We were planning for a millennium; a new and more perfect international organization would guarantee permanent peace. Under such conditions, ask Stillman and Pfaff, could Americans "have concerned themselves with the ominous encroachment of Soviet power in Eastern Europe . . .?" [4] As these writers point out, Western leaders who attempted to speak of the potential dangers of Soviet power in Eastern Europe were ignored if not "calumniated for their warnings." Such talk was considered to be dangerous propaganda that might hasten the breakup of an unstable wartime alliance.

The administration did not react more vigorously to the Soviet challenges in Eastern Europe for several reasons. The United States did not fully appreciate its own interest in Eastern Europe; we were prepared to protest the Communist take-over, but we did not consider the area worth fighting for. We also seemed unsure as to the extent that Stalin had been given a free hand in this area; and during the most crucial 1945-1946 period, there was a lack of rapport between Secretary of State Byrnes and President Truman. [5] Of great significance also was the rapid demobilization of our military strength. Rostow raises the interesting question of whether the public was really as unprepared to learn the facts and accept the need for continued strength of our armed forces as the politicians believed.[6]

Public sentiment toward the Russians at this time is quite difficult to pinpoint because, while there was great enthusiasm for the Russian struggle against the Germans, there also hovered a shadow of suspicion as to their trustworthiness. This is demonstrated by the public opinion polls. As a matter of fact, from the pre-World War II era through the immediate postwar period, public opinion vis-à-vis the Soviet Union was in a state of flux. Public sentiment for the Russians reached a low point, for example, while they were fighting the Finns, but then feelings completely reversed when the Russians successfully stemmed the German onslaught. Jerome S. Bruner writes in his study of public opinion during the war years that Russia's Communist form of government graduated "from something despicable in and of itself, to a system which we dislike but which we tolerate in Russia because Russians like it."[7]

The variation in American thinking about our relations with Russians during the war is demonstrated, too, by the observation that, from 1942 through 1945, 38 per cent to 55 per cent of a cross section of the populace thought that the Russians could be trusted.[8] This shows that even at the most favorable moments — as for example the victory at Stalingrad, the discontinuation of the Comintern, or even the Moscow or Teheran Conferences — our confidence in the Soviet Union was never overwhelming.

Before the war's end a number of incidents had aroused distrust on the part of some American officials who were on the scene and could evaluate developments at first hand.[9] Thomas A. Bailey, however, claims that the public generally was not aware of these suspicions, so that "when the war ended with an atomic bang in 1945, the American people still retained a vast reservoir of good will toward their valiant Russian ally."[10]

We had, then, a rather ambiguous view of the Russians after the war. This emphasizes the nature of the challenge which confronted President Truman when he tried to convince the American people that serious trouble was brewing between Russia and the West. Frank Freidel paints the immediate postwar scene with such broad strokes that it is of interest to quote him here: "For too many years they [the American people] had listened to publicists ranging from that advanced New Dealer Henry Wallace to the Republican president of the United States Chamber of Commerce Eric Johnston, praising the Russians and picturing Stalin as a sympathetic figure. Many had come to imagine him as a benign, pipe-smoking sage, 'good old Uncle Joe.' In addition, idealists had too long placed all their hopes upon the 'one world' which Wendell Willkie had preached so eloquently. Even long months of disturbing overseas dispatches barely dented this optimistic complacency, so badly did Americans want to believe that they could settle back to uninterrupted enjoyment of an abundant personal life in a safe unitary world." [11]

With peace on the horizon and enthusiasm for Russian military victories widespread, the public's confidence in Russia registered a highwater mark in February 1945, despite some ominous portents. Thereafter we observe a steady deterioration of public confidence in the possibility of developing a satisfactory relationship with the Soviet Union in the post-war world. One reaction was that Russia would have to do her share if cooperation between the two countries was to be maintained. Some individuals who had been sympathetic to Russia now wondered whether the time had not come to do some plain talking. Fenton describes the situation aptly: "By the end of 1945, our confidence in Russia had been severely shaken. By the end of the war, 1946, it lay completely shattered." [12]

CHAPTER X

DEMOBILIZATION

A pertinent illustration of the role of public opinion is to be found in the story of our postwar demobilization. Despite the growing suspicions of Soviet intentions during the immediate postwar period, the country proceeded with its dramatically rapid demobilization. Bailey wrote that "as in 1918, the American fire department withdrew before the fire was completely out."[1] During the last months of World War II our military power was the greatest in the world. In August 1945, our army numbered almost 8,300,000; ten months later the army had been reduced to 1,500,000 men. Due to the compelling influences on Congress, "President Truman promised that the rate of demobilization would increase to 25,000 men per day by January 1946."[2]

Because of warnings by Secretary of War Robert P. Patterson and Secretary of the Navy James V. Forrestal,[3] the President decided early in 1946 to limit the rate of discharge; but tremendous public and Congressional pressures on the administration prevented him from taking an effective stand. As Rostow has pointed out, "it would have taken extremely vigorous executive leadership, backed by a strong, well-presented case to stem the instinctive and typical American return to the ways and attitudes of peace in the months after V-J Day."[4] That the wish of the people for demobilization and normalization might possibly have been rechanneled is suggested by one analysis of the polls which indicates that during 1945-46 "a substantial American majority was prepared to keep troops in Europe and Japan, and even China; . . . that a rapid shift occurred toward reliance on United States strength rather than the UN for defense."[5]

In addition to the movement for demobilization, there was considerable opposition to compulsory military training. Forrestal had strong views on both issues. Early in the summer of 1944, he made it clear that he was concerned about the need for continued military training after the war, being very doubtful that conscription would be approved once the war was over. On August 30, 1944, he wrote to Carl Vinson, "Compulsory military service is another question which I think we have to give much attention to, and quickly. Unless we get it while the war is still in progress I for one am very skeptical whether it will ever become law."[6] In November of that year this topic was discussed with six important labor leaders in an effort to win their cooperation and support for the promotion of the idea of universal military training. A Forrestal notation dealt with a report to the Cabinet by Mr. Leo Crowley regarding his impression that the country "would be violently opposed to the continuation of any universal military training."[7]

President Truman did not lack advice on the question of military strength. For example, a State-War-Navy meeting in October 1945, concluded "that it was most inadvisable for this country to continue accelerating the demobilization of our Armed Forces at the present rate."[8] Forrestal said at this session that the situation was so grave that the President "ought to acquaint the people with the details of our dealings with the Russians and with the attitudes the Russians have manifested throughout." As in all such situations, the recommendations and pressures came not only from the official family, but from representatives of the opinion elite, the Congress, such organizations as the Women's Committee for Demobilization and the "Bring the Daddies Home" Club, as well as from impatient GI's who demanded a speedy return to civilian life.[9]

The President zealously attempted to publicize the dangers of too-rapid demobilization; but as we have shown, he was not successful and was forced to follow the dictates of the public. President Truman told me that he felt that the tide of demobilization was impossible to stem. When I suggested that this was an illustration of the determination of policy by public opinion, he did not want to admit that this was so.[10] It is entirely consistent with Truman's beliefs on leadership, expressed in Chapter VIII, that mass opinion could not in any significant way influence the administration's policies on demobilization. He might be willing to admit, however, that the circumstances called for Presidential politics. In other words, it would not be entirely accurate to say that mass opinion was the sole force behind the rapid demobilization. The President was in control; Presidential politics (Theodore Sorensen's reference to political expediency) played a major role in shaping administration policy.

In 1948 President Truman said of this immediate postwar era: "The demobilization which we carried through at that time was too fast. I tried my best to stem it, but every momma and poppa in the country had to have her boy home right immediately, and every Congressman, of course, wanted to be re-elected in 1946 and used everything he could to break up the defense program. And when we finally wound up, we had just a skeleton force in Germany, we had just a skeleton force in Japan, we had just a skeleton force in Korea. The Russians

still had four million men mobilized and under arms! And they figure
that is the difference between the carrying out of an agreement and
not carrying it out." [11]

These words are certainly an admission that head long demobilization served to restrain American foreign policy; hence it was urgent
that the people be made aware of the facts. A letter written to the
White House in October 1945, less than three months after Truman's
return from Potsdam, shows an active administration plan to diminish
the rate of demobilization. Addressed to Matthew J. Connelly, Secretary to the President, by Richard L. Davies, Chairman of the
Foreign Policy Association, the letter indicates that the President
had taken steps to influence public sentiment. The sections quoted
below deal with these points:

"In accordance with the President's request when I talked with him
Monday I presented the appeal for the people to reconsider this too
hasty demobilization in Europe, over station WFIL Monday night,
and at a Foreign Policy Association meeting Tuesday noon, at which
former Supreme Court Justice Owen J. Roberts presided. Justice
Roberts, Mr. Harrison and I went on station WIP Tuesday night and
I presented the same appeal. Finally last night I presented it over
187 stations of the ABC network.

"In the radio talks I also asked that the people write the President
on this critical question of speed of demobilization in Europe and
I would anticipate that an appreciable amount of mail on the subject
would be coming into the White House. In order that this 'trial balloon' may be of most value to the President I wonder if you would
arrange to have your mail analysis people be on the lookout for
communications on this particular subject so that the President can
get a clear picture of public reaction." [12]

A letter from Governor Thye of Minnesota to the President on
December 11, 1945, served as a catalyst for Executive action because
it elucidated Truman's problem at that particular time. Governor
Thye expressed understanding of the public's desire to have the boys
home again as soon as possible. But he also suggested that, "There
could be formulated public explanations of policy and need that
would lift the veil of uncertainty from the hearts of anxiously waiting
families, and make clear the tasks that remain to be done. . . ." On
December 14, 1945, the following memorandum was prepared for
the Secretary of War by Samuel I. Rosenman. "The President would
like to make a statement along the lines suggested by Governor Thye
of Minnesota in the attached letter. Could you have someone prepare

a draft of such a statement in consultation with someone from the Navy Department?" Subsequently, a memorandum was forwarded to Judge Rosenman on December 22, 1945, from Secretary of War Robert P. Patterson. This memorandum was edited by Rosenman, and a final statement was issued on January 8, 1946, in which the President said that demobilization would be carried out with all possible speed. However, Truman also emphasized that we now had to assume our "full share of responsibility for keeping the peace and destroying the war-making potential of the hostile nations that were bent on keeping the world in a state of warfare." By this time the critical need for troops overseas had already slowed the Army's rate of demobilization. The President was therefore laying the groundwork for his long and arduous campaign to convince the public that the nation had an inescapable responsibility to carry out "its obligation in this difficult and critical postwar period in which we must devote all necessary strength to building a firm foundation for the future peace of the world. The future of our country now is as much at stake as it was in the days of the war." [15]

CHAPTER XI

FOCUS ON CRISIS TENSIONS

Before we can examine the impact of public opinion on President Truman's decisions in the early postwar period, we must understand his personal attitudes at this time. Six months after Yalta and only three months after his inauguration, he left for Potsdam where he had his first contact with the Russians. On the basis of comments he made regarding this conference, it is difficult to establish with any accuracy what his views of the Soviet Union were. Apparently he was very much on his guard but continued to be optimistic about the future. A number of important issues were settled at Pottsdam, and Truman received personal reaffirmation from Stalin that Russia would participate in the war against Japan. Yet he writes: "I was not altogether disillusioned to find now that the Russians were not in earnest about peace. It was clear that the Russian foreign policy was based on the conclusion that we were heading for a major depression, and they were already planning to take advantage of our setback." [1]

Truman claims that it was his experience at Potsdam that led him to exclude the Russians from control in Japan; "Force," he emphasizes, "is the only thing the Russians understand." Yet in 1949 the President referred to the atmosphere at Potsdam as cordial and pleasant. He noted that he had left there "with the idea that we would have no difficulty whatever in attaining a settlement when the war should have been completely won." And he admitted that it took a year and a half after Potsdam until "we all came to the conclusion that agreements were made by one for the express purpose of breaking them." [2] It was only after the Potsdam Conference, Truman stated in 1960, that the Russians "began breaking agreements with us regarding Germany and Poland and Rumania and Bulgaria." At this point, he declared, "I began to feel we were up against something we had to meet." He had hoped, like many others, that the Russians would keep their agreements. When they broke them, "we had to do the best we could." [3]

On his first day in office the President received a memorandum stating that "since the Yalta Conference the Soviet Government has taken a firm and uncompromising position on nearly every major question that has arisen in our relations." [4] Secretary of State Stettinius, briefing the President for the first time, informed him of the difficulties that hampered our negotiations with the Russians. Also, before President Truman went to Potsdam he had a confrontation with Molotov over Poland; and it is clear from conversations that the President had with Harriman and others that he intended to be firm in his dealings with the Soviet Union. He noted that he had admired the Russians' courage in face of the tremendous losses they had suffered during the war, and he said that he "was in a mood to do anything in the world to help them — help them recover."[5] He therefore went to the Potsdam Conference "with the kindliest of feelings in the world towards the Russians," and he was satisfied when he returned home because they had promised to enter the Pacific war three months after Germany's defeat. The President on several occasions also declared that "Old Joe" was "not a bad guy" and invited him to visit the United States.

After the Potsdam Conference, however, President Truman sensed that Soviet foreign policy decisions had increasingly fallen into the hands of Molotov and Vishinsky; and finally he came to the realization that the agreements made at Potsdam would not be carried out. Those in responsible positions who dealt with the Russians encountered their all too frequent "Niet." In the President's words "I found out and I came to the conclusion, as I think everybody else who has had any direct dealings with the Russians, that they respect force. They do not respect anything else." Truman made one broad statement which indicates how sentiment toward the Soviet Union was revised: "Our policy over a year and a half gradually changed to one of meeting them head-on, and telling them exactly what we would agree to, and standing by it. We are still following that policy. That is the only policy you can follow with them. I am of the opinion that if we follow through with a proper preparedness program, which I have asked Congress to give us, we will eventually get the peace we all pray for."[6]

Indicative of a mood which was later to be more widespread throughout the country was the President's encounter with Molotov prior to the San Francisco Conference. Though Secretary of War Stimson had urged caution, Truman spoke very firmly and told Molotov, according to Forrestal, "that if one part of the agreement which they had entered with President Roosevelt at Yalta were breached . . . the entire Yalta agreement was no longer binding on any of the parties interested."[7] The Special Assistant to the Secretary of State, Mr. Bohlen, who attended the meetings between the two men, has confirmed that Truman was quite tough. He described the attitude of the President, after less than two weeks in office, in these words: "The President said . . . that he felt our agreements with the Soviet Union so far had been a one-way street and that he could not continue; it was now or never. He intended to go on with the plans for San Francisco and if the Russians did not wish to join us they could go to hell . . ."[8]

We may conclude that there was a hardening of the Administration's attitude toward the Soviet Union over a year and a half. The record shows that insofar as specific incidents are concerned Truman did not hesitate to adopt a firm tone, particularly on the advice of such men as Harriman and Forrestal. The main goal of our policy, however, was to win the confidence of the Soviet leaders; hence our policy continued to be a very flexible one.

It is noteworthy that, even before the menace of the Soviet Union was fully appreciated, President Truman was laying the groundwork for the transition of public opinion to support of America's new role in international affairs. Long before the policy of containment was formulated, the President was emphasizing our new responsibility in the postwar world; and he continued to do so effectively throughout his administration whenever the opportunity presented itself, particularly in the Middle West.

The Second World War had brought about a remarkable change of sentiment regarding America's position of leadership, but this sentiment had to be reinforced by the Executive. The President was, therefore, entitled to state in 1960: "We transformed the policy of the country from isolationism into internationalism. If you don't think that was a job, you ought to try it sometime."[9] President Truman repeatedly spoke about the need for strength and leadership, and not in response to the aggressive policy of the Soviet Union or the extreme demands of the proponents of demobilization. In an excellent address broadcast nationally the President said on April 6, 1946: "The United States today is a strong nation; there is none stronger. This is not a boast. It is a fact, which calls for solemn thought and due humility. It means that with such strength, we have to assume the leadership and accept responsibility. . . . We still have much to do. We are determined to remain strong." He added that the U.S. expected other major powers to pursue peaceful objectives. Recognizing the critical needs of other areas, he noted that "we shall help because we know that we ourselves cannot enjoy prosperity in a world of economic stagnation."[10]

In his State of the Union Message, January 6, 1947, Truman mentioned no problem concerning the Soviet Union except that it had been difficult to reach agreement on the peace treaties for Italy, Bulgaria, Rumania, and Hungary. However, he made a good case for a strong United States. His main theme was stated as follows: "This is an age when unforeseen attack could come with unprecedented speed. We must be strong enough to defeat, and thus forestall, any such attack. In our steady progress toward a more rational world order, the need for large armed forces is progressively declining; but the stabilizing force of American military strength must not be weakened until our hopes are fully realized."

President Truman continued to emphasize that isolationism was dead. He did not hesitate to take this message into what had once been known as isolationist territory. Typical of his views were these words: "Many of our people, here in America, used to think that we could escape the troubles of the world by simply staying within our own borders. Two wars have shown how wrong they were. We know today that we cannot find security in isolation. If we are to live at peace, we must join with other nations in a continuing effort to organize the world for peace."[11] Describing those who wanted the U.S. to pull out of all joint efforts, reverse our foreign policy and retire behind our own defense as isolationists, the President referred to them as "dangerous not only to the cause of world peace, but also to our *own* national security." In vigorously attacking the arguments presented by the isolationists, he said: "Isolationism is the road to war. Worse than that, isolationism is the road to defeat in war. The people who are striving to destroy our foreign aid programs and our programs for the common defense of the free nations, are striking at our own national security. They may not mean to do us harm, but they are as dangerous to our future as those who deliberately plot against our freedom."[12]

These words indicated President Truman's awareness of the strong isolationist minority remaining on the political scene.

CHAPTER XII

THE CITIZENRY ALERTED

We have seen that early in 1945 the American people counted on the friendship of the Soviet Union in the postwar world. "Seven out of ten Americans," as John Fenton has pointed out, "favored the idea of sending German men to Russia to help rebuild her war-shattered cities. Only a negligible minority of 6 per cent of the public was disappointed in the results of the Yalta Conference. Less than one year later, the picture had sharply changed."[1]

The policies pursued in the Eastern European countries, the Russian position in Iran, the Gouzenka spy case, and other incidents were disillusioning to many. By the middle of 1946, "nearly six out of ten Americans diagnosed Russia's intentions as those of a nation building up *the* ruling power in the world." He points out the striking change in public opinion which occurred when he writes "there are certainly few instances in the nation's history where public opinion has been literally *forced* to make such a complete about-face."[2]

Stalin delivered an important speech on February 9, 1946. American reaction to it indicates the indecisiveness of public opinion at this time. The speech was carefully scrutinized for indications of future Soviet policy. It was clear that the Russians had not yet lost their suspicions of the West. Premier Stalin called for Bolshevist vigilance backed by tremendous armaments against any eventuality, and he stated that the two World Wars were the inevitable result of the development of world economic and political forces based on monopoly capitalism. He announced a new Five-Year Plan and forecast the tripling and quadrupling of Russia's output of pig iron, coal, steel, and oil within the next fifteen years. And he predicted that Russia would surpass other countries in scientific achievement. Fear gripped the hearts of many as they read these ambitious plans.

This speech was a reaffirmation of Russia's historic suspicion of the West. Analysts noted particularly that Stalin made no mention of lend-lease aid nor of the United Nations. There was no reference to peaceful coexistence nor to the idea that capitalism and communism could find a meeting ground for cooperation toward world peace. The only hopeful sign a *New York Times* editorial could find was that despite "this new Russian policy and party line, the situation had this helpful aspect — that Russia has been collaborating with the socialist and capitalist countries in the United Nations Organization. As long as that collaboration continues, there remains the hope that the doctrine and policy of any party will bow to the supreme issue of maintaining the world's peace."[3]

There was wide divergence in the comments of editors, columnists, and radio commentators. Some influential journalists who had tended to be sympathetic to the Soviet Union were disturbed by Stalin's emphasis on military power. And reactions differed to the announced program of industrialization. Dorothy Thompson wrote that there was nothing in what Stalin had said which "had not been made abundantly plain" by Russian practice, and she claimed our officials had to have their noses rubbed into reality before they can see it. A few commentators (e.g., Constantine Brown, Earl Godwin) stated that the speech was "merely a fulfillment of their own predictions." Of greatest interest is the response of those who previously had been hopeful that the wartime coalition would produce peacetime collaboration with Russia. It seemed to some of these commentators (Marquis Childs, Whaley-Eaton) that "Stalin's speech closed the door"; Newsweek and Time referred to the speech as the "most warlike pronouncement uttered by any statesman since V-J Day."

However, other journals (PM, Nation, St. Louis Post-Dispatch) saw nothing disturbing in the Soviet industrialization program. The Post-Dispatch and the Des Moines Register berated those who wanted to "stop Russia" from outdoing us economically and ask why we should be "horrified" that Russia wants a steel industry "commensurate with her size, population and natural resources." Some "middle-of-the-road" newspapers (Kansas City Star, Nashville Tennessean, Newark News and Birmingham Age-Herald) were convinced that Russia only wanted to promote her internal development. The New Orleans Times-Picayune and Minneapolis Tribune stated that we should continue to promote our development as well as build up our strength for any eventuality.

Others who considered Stalin's pronouncements a clear challenge to the West are Raymond Swing, Walter Lippmann, and Sumner Welles. Lippmann suggested that we begin military discussions with the Soviet Union for the purpose of regulating armaments and outlawing weapons, including the bomb; Welles deplored American weakness compared with Russian power and warned Americans to heed the lessons of 1919 and 1939. Perhaps most typical of the responses was the combination of hope and self-interest expressed by the St. Louis Post-Dispatch. The answer to Russia's military might, said this paper, was "to keep ourselves strong while working with her in the UNO."

Little more than two weeks after the widespread reporting of and reaction to Stalin's speech, the doubts which had begun to affect some people were expressed by two Americans of prominence. An address delivered by Senator Vandenberg on the floor of the Senate after his return from the first meeting of the United Nations in London[4] covered the whole session, but one quotation adequately summarizes the theme of his remarks. Referring to Vishinsky's[5] stubborn and aggressive behavior in the first meeting of the Security Council, Senator Vandenberg said it posed the same question in his mind that he had found in every newspaper he read — namely — "What is Russia up to now?" . . . "We ask it in Manchuria. We ask it in eastern Europe and the Dardanelles." We ask it, Senator Vandenberg continued, with reference to Italy, Iran, Tripolitania, the Baltic and the Balkans, Poland, the capital of Canada, and Japan. "We ask it sometimes even in connection with events in our own United States." And he added with disquieting frankness, that he "sensed at London what seemed to be too great a tendency to relapse into power politics, and, in greater or less degree to use the United Nations as a self-serving tribune rather than as tribunal."

Secretary of State James F. Byrnes, also reporting to the nation on the London meeting, expressed the desire of the United States to continue "on terms of friendship and partnership with the Soviet Union"; but he bluntly warned that this country "cannot allow aggression to be accomplished by coercion or pressure by subterfuges such as political infiltration." Byrnes continued "I should be lacking in candor if I said to you that world conditions today are sound or reassuring. All around us there is suspicion and distrust which in turn breeds suspicion and distrust." Speaking only one day after Senator Vandenberg, Byrnes said that ideological barriers should not prevent the United States and the Soviet Union from living peacefully together in the same world, but he added: "We will not and we cannot stand aloof if force or the threat of force is used contrary to the purposes and principles of the [United Nations] Charter. America is a great power and we must act as a great power."[6]

A New York Times editorial stated: "Taken together, these two speeches must be considered as ushering in a new orientation in American international relations." There is no doubt that the words of these two men inspired a careful scrutiny and redefinition of American foreign policy.

Anne O'Hare McCormick headlined her column after Byrnes' address: "The Stiffening Attitude Toward Russia." It was her feeling that he "was undoubtedly responding to a rising popular demand when he broadcast from the Overseas Press Club the most forthright statement the administration has made of the American attitude toward the bewildering developments in the international field." Noting that Americans were beginning to worry, she stated that they are filled with "a vague sense of foreboding." Commenting on Byrnes' special qualifications, she declared: "Mr. Byrnes' long experience in domestic politics make him peculiarly sensitive to home opinion, and perhaps the most significant thing about his forceful address is that he thought it was what the country wanted and was waiting to hear." She summarized the public attitude as follows: "What does Russia want? How far will she go, and what is the American answer to her claims? These are the questions crystallizing in the vague fear and confusion. The same citizens who clamored for the boys to come home are now beginning to press for an 'American stand.' "

Miss McCormick pointed out that Byrnes' stronger stand "against unilateral action by any power will lead the Russians to interpret his speech as an expression of American sentiment" not only because Senator Vandenberg and John F. Dulles [7] had issued a call for plain speaking, but particularly because the Secretary of State previously had been playing the role of conciliator in the Security Council as well as at the Foreign Ministers Conference in Moscow.

Tom Connally, Chairman of the Senate Foreign Relations Committee, supported Byrnes' new emphasis on strength by recommending a return to universal military training in a report to the Senate. Strengthening sentiments previously expressed, he said that any policy of patience and firmness must be anchored to "an adequate Army, a superior Navy and a superlative Air Force. We shall not maintain these armed forces for aggression or conquest. They must be maintained for our security, for the defense of our people, our territories. They must be maintained to sustain our international rights and obligations. They must be maintained to resist any aggressor who may threaten our security or any plan or scheme for world conquest. These purposes are not inconsistent with our loyalty and devotion to the United Nations." [8]

James Reston observed that the addresses of Vandenberg and Byrnes indicated a trend: "Speeches which have started out as mere speeches have often turned into policies when they were generally approved, as this one has been." [9] Correspondents such as Barnet Nover, the Alsops, Dorothy Thompson, and Paul Mallon, analyzing the Soviet moves, were demanding a "get tough with Russia" policy. Other observers (e.g., Murrow, Shirer, Matthews and Sulzberger of the *New York Times*) had previously commented on the conflict of outlook between Russia and the Western Powers. Many of these observers were insisting that "Russia must be stopped now before it is too late." Walter Lippmann suggested that the problem was much more complicated than it appeared by raising the question of whether we should appease or resist Russian expansion. The main issue, he felt, was how we could bolster China, Great Britain, and Western Europe. [10] Commentators began to write about the need for "translating words into actions" particularly with reference to the need for Congressional action on the British loan, European relief, and our own military establishment.

The cautionary speeches were all delivered during the period when Russia failed to withdraw her troops from Iran by the scheduled date of March 2. Together they contributed powerfully to the shaping of a public opinion which demanded greater firmness in our contacts with the Russians. The Scripps-Howard papers, reflecting this point of view, commented: "A show-down is inevitable . . . the only hope is in convincing Russia that the price of her aggression is eventually another world war." [11]

Aroused by Stalin's speech on February 9, further alerted by the reports to the nation of the American United Nations delegates (Vandenberg, Byrnes, and to a lesser degree Connally and Dulles), public reaction reached its climax in the dramatic response to the speech delivered by Winston Churchill at Fulton, Missouri, on March 5, 1946. In retrospect, this address was the high point of the foreign policy debate which took place in 1946. The background to this speech is well known; nevertheless, there are a number of questions which are difficult to answer.

Frank L. McCluer, President of Westminster College, managed to arrange a speaking engagement for Winston Churchill at the College through Harry Vaughan, President Truman's aide. The invitation was endorsed by the President; and Churchill, who was then vacationing in Florida, accepted it, indicating that he welcomed this opportunity to address the American people. The speech was surrounded with considerable publicity since the President accompanied Churchill to Fulton; this in itself should indicate that the President fully supported the message there delivered by Churchill.

Churchill's address has come to be known as the "Iron Curtain" speech, a term he first used, therein: "From Stettin in the Baltic to Trieste in the Adriatic an iron curtain has descended across the Continent . . . I do not believe that Soviet Russia desires war. What they desire is the fruits of war and the indefinite expansion of their power and doctrines. . . . From what I have seen of our Russian friends and allies during the war, I am convinced that there is nothing for which they have less respect than for weakness, especially military weakness." [12]

Churchill's warning bolstered American spokesmen who had suggested that perhaps peace was as near at hand as so many believed; and his words particularly affected those who believed that the United Nations would be able to solve all the world's problems. The most effective way of confronting the Soviet Union, Churchill thought, was to build a firm Anglo-American alliance whose foundation would be "the growing friendship and mutual understanding" between the two countries. [13]

There is a difference of opinion about the effect of Churchill's words on the public. On the one hand, there was the feeling that he "presented an analysis which is very much in line with American thinking." [14] Other observers disagreed totally. Frank Freidel said: "Not even the revered Churchill could shift American opinion." [15] Eric Goldman wrote that Churchill's doctrine "brought few cheers in Fulton or anywhere else in the United States." [16]

Given the general setting and dramatic content of this speech, the coverage and analysis by the press were somewhat disappointing. Most of the comments and criticisms were reserved for Churchill's discussion of the feasibility of a "fraternal association" between Great Britain and the United States rather than with his remarks which dealt with the Soviet Union. Even the New York Times' attitude was cautious, saying that the "acceptability and desirability" of Churchill's proposal "for a military alliance" must await the future course of events. The hesitancy of the editor in supporting this proposal was based on the premise that we should be reluctant "to take any action which might tend to jeopardize or to weaken the prestige of the UNO. . . ." [17] This thought continued to serve as an indirect but important restraint on our policy.

Just as it is difficult to determine the true impact of Churchill's speech on the American public, it is equally difficult to determine President Truman's reaction to it. "The world," observed Herbert Agar, "was surprised by the frankness with which Sir Winston in the heart of the isolationist Missouri Valley, named the Russian danger and called for an Anglo-American alliance to halt the 'expansive tendencies' of the Soviet. But the President was not surprised. He had passed through and outlived his own stage of thinking that the former Prime Minister was merely an old-fashioned imperialist who fretted unnecessarily about the 'Eastern question.' Yet he may well have been astonished by the severity with which the American public adhered in 1946 to the Truman views of 1945. Astonished or not, he met the widespread and bitter attacks on Sir Winston's speech with his customary refusal to retreat. 'I knew what he was going to say . . . I didn't care what he said. We pretend to believe in free speech, don't we.' " [18]

Frank Freidel had this to say about the speech and its after effects: "President Truman had intended Churchill's admonition as a trial balloon; it collapsed miserably. It frightened the public much as had Roosevelt's 'quarantine speech' nine years earlier. Yet Americans accepted "iron curtain" as part of their new vocabulary, and slowly, reluctantly, switched toward the view it implied. Within six months they were jeering Wallace, whose fervent adherence to the 'one world' philosophy led him out of Truman's cabinet and into public denunciation of American foreign policy. Within a year after the 'iron curtain' speech, President Truman, with the support of the American people was fabricating a new strong stand against Russian encroachment." [19]

Eric Goldman has noted that Truman is supposed to have said that the speech was a trial balloon which had given him "an unmistakable view of public opinion," [20] but Jonathan Daniels has suggested another interpretation of the President's views: "A feeling against appeasement undoubtedly entered into the fact of his presence on the platform at Westminster College, Fulton, Missouri, in March, when Private Citizen Churchill spoke of the 'expansive tendencies' of the Soviets and called for an Anglo-American alliance to halt them. Truman still insists, however, that his relationship to the Fulton speech was based upon neighborly impulse and not international relations. He was joining in a build-up for Westminster, the alma mater of his lively military aide Vaughan, and not on a pattern of foreign affairs."

Daniels added: "It did not displease him [Truman] to have the eloquent bluntness of Churchill sound from the platform on which he sat in Missouri." [21] President Truman himself makes only an indirect reference to the address. The comments by Daniels, though the least dramatic of the evaluations that I have seen, may well come closest to the truth. The speech served as an additional signpost on the way to a new outlook on the world. But the President was undoubtedly aware of the lack of enthusiasm with which Churchill's statements were received by many.

Diametrically opposed opinions on the speech could be found among Congressmen, for instance. Senators Pepper of Florida, Kilgore of West Virginia, and Taylor of Idaho issued a joint statement saying, "Mr. Churchill's proposal would cut the throat of the United Nations Organization. It would destroy the unity of the Big Three, without which the war could not have been won and without which the peace cannot be saved." [22] This was, however, very definitely a minority viewpoint on Capitol Hill.

Six months after Churchill had attempted to alert America, the country witnessed another great debate when Henry Wallace, then Secretary of Commerce, charged that we had not been trying to meet Russia halfway. At this time neither the views of Churchill nor of Wallace were acceptable to the American people. They generally continued to have faith in the United Nations as the solution to all problems, although there was some support for a tougher line against the Soviet Union, in spite of an evident reluctance to provide the means for such a policy.

In the autumn of 1946, when the whole question of developing a firmer policy toward the Soviet Union had been thoroughly discussed publicly, a public opinion survey showed that 63 per cent were asking for a "greater willingness" to meet Russia's views, 12 per cent indicated satisfaction with our policy, 8 per cent opposed further cooperation with the Russians, and 6 per cent indicated "no opinion." A few newspapers of regional importance suggested that a policy of "toughness" had not proven itself; the Federal Council of Churches suggested a program for the improvement of Soviet-American relations.[23] In addition there were the always vocal but limited supporters of Henry Wallace, The New Republic, Nation, Max Lerner, the American Labor Party, and a number of CIO spokesmen. On the whole however, the polls indicated a steady decline in the belief that it was possible to cooperate with the Russians. A year later the majority opinion was 3 to 1 against the proposition that we can "count on Russia half-way in working out problems together." [24]

Any study of mass opinion in connection with foreign policy must be highly speculative at best. Except for rare occasions, it is not even possible to speak of the existence of mass opinion, and we know that its staying-power is usually limited. We also must realize that conflicting data makes firm conclusions about the state of the public mind at any one time very difficult. Nevertheless, we have attempted to make some generalizations for the 1946 period, a time when opinion was in a particular state of flux.

A study of public attitudes by the Survey Research Center demonstrates that there was a greater distrust and more criticism of the Soviet Union than we have indicated.[25] These findings are summarized here only to emphasize how tenuous our own conclusions must be. In the table cited below, note particularly the high percentage of *No's* and *No's* with qualifications or uncertainty:

Do you think that the Russian government is trying to cooperate with the rest of the world as much as it can?

	June*	August*	December
Yes	3%	2%	4%
Yes, with qualifications or uncertainty	10	7	15
Undecided, don't know	14	15	14
No, with qualifications or uncertainty	21	12	24
No	49	61	42
Opinions not ascertained	3	3	1
No. of cases	100	100	100

*Data for June and August are from surveys of comparable samples conducted by the SRC.

Subsequent to the debate on how tough[26] we should be with the Soviet Union, the question of American aid to Greece and Turkey was of vital importance in molding public attitudes toward administration policy. Discussion of this aid program reached proportions which reminded many observers of the 1940-1941 debate over the American stake in the European war. The wide-ranging coverage in the public information media, the debates in Congress, and the opinion polls all indicated that a solid majority favored the plan. We should note that this issue was the first to be discussed within the context of halting further Soviet aggression, and it is sometimes suggested that much public support was generated on the basis of this argument.

Surveys indicated that although there was good public support for the economic and financial aspects of the program to aid Greece and Turkey, there was reluctance to grant military assistance. At the height of the debate, just prior to enactment of the Greek-Turkish aid bill in both houses of Congress, a survey showed that the public, by a ratio of 2½ to 1, supported providing funds to Greece to help her "recover from the war"; but over half this cross-section of the public was reluctant to make military supplies available to Greece (53% to 37%) and Turkey (54% to 30%) To underline some of the dramtic inconsistencies in the public mind, 40% of the same cross section indicated that the United Nations should have been allowed to play a more significant role in regard to the problem of those nations. A cry for firmness and toughness seems to be accompanied by a yearning to escape direct responsibility for taking action. By February 1948, however, the public was recorded as being in sympathy with the supply of military aid by a 2 to 1 majority.

Public approval of the Marshall Plan illustrated the new world-consciousness. A comparison of one hundred newspaper editorials that appeared immediately after Marshall's Harvard address showed support of 10 to 1 for the program presented.[27] With some exceptions (Hearst, *Chicago Tribune*) it was not a question of whether we should aid Europe, but rather: "how much, how soon, and in what way."[28] (The impressive work of the Committee for the Marshall Plan will be discussed in the next chapter.)

A third important issue which called for public debate was the North Atlantic Security Pact. Its overwhelming enactment by the Congress should not obscure the fact that the most searching questions had to be answered before public approval was won. However, by the summer of 1949, when the Senate was ready to vote, a survey showed that 77 per cent of a cross section expressed approval of the pact. Approximately 10 per cent disapproved, while 13 per cent gave no opinion.[29]

There is no indication that the public was prepared in 1950 to reduce its support for a firm policy toward the Soviet Union. A survey by the NORC showed that 67 per cent of a nation-wide cross section approved the statement that "we should be even firmer than we are today" in our negotiations with the U.S.S.R. Only 9 per cent suggested that we should demonstrate more willingness to compromise; 15 per cent said that our current policy was about right, and 9 per cent gave no opinion.[30] It is no surprise, therefore, that President Truman received almost unanimous support for his response to the Communist challenge in Korea. The outbreak of the Korean conflict had a notable effect on the public's outlook on other issues, particularly with regard to policies in Western Europe. Two NORC polls indicated an increased appreciation of the need for a strong defensive position in Western Europe.[31]

	Pre-Korea	Per cent Approving July
North Atlantic Treaty	81	87
Arms Aid to Western Europe	62	73
Continuation of Marshall Plan	56	64
Creation of West German Army	40	54

To convey the general atmosphere in which foreign policy decisions have to be made, we may cite one other illustration of how difficult it is to make any accurate judgments regarding the temper of the public. Although there was popular approval of the American action in Korea — the polls in October of 1950 record that 81 per cent felt that President Truman was right in sending troops, and a majority of Americans supported the proposal that our forces cross the 38th parallel — a differing conclusion must be drawn from an opinion study issued three months later. It showed in February 1951, that the "isolationist" viewpoint was still represented by one out of every four Americans, who thought that it would be "best for the future" if the United States stayed "out of world affairs." [32] As we have shown in the previous chapter, President Truman was aware of this segment of the public, and he deliberately directed his efforts to inform and alert it to America's new position of leadership.

Chapter XIII

THE MARSHALL PLAN AND KOREA

Hans J. Morgenthau refers to the years between 1945 and 1947 as the "deadly hiatus" because they were filled with "erroneous thinking, inarticulate action, and untoward results. . . ." By 1947, however, our foreign policy was becoming more positive and constructive. This new trend "manifested itself in three political innovations: containment, the Truman Doctrine, and the Marshall Plan."[1]

The latter two programs exemplify President Truman's belief that his major task was the making of original decisions. He felt that if the decision was right, the people, once made aware of the facts, would support him. Robert Elder has quoted Secretary of State Marshall as saying that "no policy—foreign or domestic can succeed without public support."[2]

The task, however, was not as simple as it might have seemed. The various objections and suspicions these two new programs generated among the public and in the Congress have been catalogued by Barbara Ward. They included criticism of the President for not relying on the United Nations, "for embarking on unnecessary world crusades, for wasting American dollars and taking the first step towards wasting American men." In reference to the Truman Doctrine she observes "the figure [$400,000,000] was finally voted—unwillingly and grudgingly amid a general feeling of drift and indecision."[3]

Louis J. Halle has observed that the Europeans and the British, though elated at the results, were also somewhat shocked "by the verbal bluntness of our approach." Halle explains our behaviour in the following way: "I think . . . that this may have been a necessity in the relations between our government and our people. In 1947, as in 1917 and 1941, we had to have our emotions aroused by the combination of a great crisis and a great cause if we were going to support the action that had to be taken."[4]

The challenge of winning support for the Greek-Turkish aid program has sometimes been underestimated. The responsibility for maintaining order in the world had shifted too quickly for the public to comprehend. Most Americans were not aware of the background that explained the events making this aid necessary. Many members of Congress were "grim and resentful." There was a tendency to blame the British "for going broke and passing the baton to us."

Influential members of Congress like Senators Robert A. Taft (Ohio) and Harry F. Byrd (Virginia) objected to military loans as well as the sending of military advisors.[5]

With regard to the crisis in Greece, the State Department set in motion consulting and planning procedures more rapidly than usual. One reason may be that the Department had been following British economic developments closely and therefore grasped the significance of the British White Paper issued at the beginning of 1947. Thus, Britain's announcement of the withdrawal of support from Greece and Turkey did not come as a complete surprise.

On February 24, 1947, the British Ambassador officially informed the State Department of the decision to withdraw. Consultations took place between the Secretary of State and President Truman, as well as with the Secretaries of War and of the Navy, and the Chiefs of Staff. The administration decided to take over Britain's responsibility. Congressional leaders, however, had not yet been consulted. A meeting for this purpose was called at the White House on February 27th. Mr. Dean Acheson, the Under-Secretary of State, and Secretary of State Marshall[6] explained the recent developments to the Congressional leaders.

According to a memorandum prepared by Joseph M. Jones, then an assistant to the Assistant Secretary for Public Affairs, "the reaction of the Congressional leaders was rather trivial."[7] Mr. Acheson emphasized the importance of Greece and Turkey to our own security, particularly in view of the pressures exerted throughout the world by the Communists. The time had come to take a firm stand. "Most of the Congressional leaders" Jones pointed out, "were greatly shaken and impressed with this analysis and promised to support whatever measures should be necessary, *on the condition* that the President should explain the situation fully to Congress in a special message, and to the people by radio. They felt that they could support such a program only if the public were appraised of the grim facts. The President promised to go to the Congress and the people in this manner."[8] At the end of the memorandum Jones said that "we all felt bowled over by the gravity of the situation and the immensity of the steps that were contemplated."

The significant problem for the President, when it become evident that aid for Greece had become an issue in American policy, was not whether we would act to restrain expanding communism, but how to convince the Congress and the people that an aid program was necessary. The Secretary and Under-Secretary of State, other members of the Cabinet, and Senator Vandenberg° emphasized the importance of working out a program that would command public support. This was the essential challenge confronting the President and his administration. On February 28th a meeting of the Subcommittee on Foreign Policy Information of the State-War-Navy Coordinating Committee considered these problems. The Committee concluded that, in addition to gathering political, economic, and military data on the aid program it would be necessary to "set out informational objectives, draft the themes to be used in the public approach, consider what the lines of Soviet propaganda would be and how to counter them, and prepare specific informational programs for getting the story over to the press, radio, magazines, and group leaders throughout the country." [10]

Within the State Department itself a paper was prepared dealing with the informational objectives and the main themes of American policy. The principal objectives were summarized as follows:

"1. To make possible the formulation of intelligent opinions by the American people on the problems created by the present situation in Greece through the furnishing of full and frank information by the Government.

"2. To portray the world conflict between free and totalitarian or imposed forms of government.

"3. To bring about an understanding by the American people of the world strategic situation." [11]

A complete program of public information was planned by the State Department. While some of the techniques mentioned below are fairly standard, it is interesting to see the variety of activities that are involved. Some of the techniques employed in this situation were utilized for later programs. The program included the following:

"(a) A schedule of press conferences for the Secretary of State with journalists.

"(b) A series of background meetings programmed for an especially qualified group of speakers from the Department.

"(c) Specially arranged meetings with the representatives of different news media (i.e. press club luncheons).

"(d) Written material to be prepared for mass distribution (fact sheets, background summaries, reprints of major speeches).

"(e) Make arrangements to get subject discussed on radio as much as possible; suggest speakers for interview programs.

"(f) Arrange meetings with organization representatives.

"(g) Invite magazine editors and feature writers for background meetings; help to develop articles, editorials, and other materials for general and specialized audiences.

"(h) Plan speaking programs for Department speakers throughout the country, directed toward 'leadership audiences.' " [12]

James Forrestal, commenting on a Cabinet meeting which took place on March 7, 1947, said that "the general consensus of the Cabinet was that we should support Greece to the extent that we can persuade Congress and the country of the necessity." Forrestal underlines the President's direct involvement in the planning of the educational campaign. Toward the end of the meeting, he reports, "the President appointed a committee headed by John Snyder, including Harriman, Patterson, Acheson and myself to lay out a program of communication with leaders throughout the country and particularly of the plan for laying the facts before a selected group of business people. I said this selection should be made most carefully; that simply a conventional and well-advertised gathering of big shots was not what we wanted—we had to reach men who were active in business and who would have to do the job." [13]

Effective leadership erased the original hesitancy in the public mind, and the bill to aid Greece and Turkey was approved by heavy majorities in the Senate and the House (67-23; 287-107); the President signed the bill on May 22, 1947.

The same strategy had to be employed for the Marshall Plan. Secretary of State Marshall and his advisors agreed that announcement of the plan to make economic aid available to Europe had to be timed carefully: "It had to break with 'explosive force,' he believed, to overcome isolationist opposition. 'The feeling seemed to be,' he explained in a later memorandum, 'that any new proposal for more funds to be appropriated would be ruthlessly repulsed. Therefore, the manner of statement, the first approach, and similar factors had to be most seriously considered. It is easy to propose a great plan, but exceedingly difficult to manage the form and procedure so that it has a fair chance of political survival.' " [14]

Dean Acheson's Delta Council speech was one of the steps that led to the writing of the Secretary of State's address for the Harvard University Commencement on June 5, 1947. Lippmann, summarizing what the administration had in mind after Mr. Acheson's speech wrote: "The Administration will do well to address itself to the adult and informed population of the United States, and to assume that the American people would rather hear the truth than be jazzed up and needled by rhetoric, and that they will do their duty when they are presented with a well prepared plan for discharging their duty."

Lippmann also quoted James Reston's observation that "the Administration is not happy about the emotional response here and abroad to the military and ideological aspects of the Truman Doctrine." According to Lippmann, the anti-Communist sales pitch, in attempting to win support for President Truman's program, had detracted from the real merits of the idea. He expressed the hope that similar emphasis could be avoided in the development of a massive aid-program for Western Europe.[15]

A vast amount of work was done under the leadership of the President to win public support for the Marshall Plan. The Council of Economic Advisors were directed to make a study, and other committees were set up to evaluate programs which Congress might approve. Most important of these committees was the President's Committee on Foreign Aid (Harriman Committee) which did much of the spadework for the program. This was an advisory group of nineteen "distinguished citizens" representing different facets of American life.[16] Price notes that Senator Vandenberg had suggested the advisory council during a bipartisan consultation at the White House, where upon Dean Acheson took the initiative in setting up the Committee.

Some of the difficulties the administration encountered in pushing the Marshall Plan were outlined by Senator Vandenberg: "The Marshall idea fell upon a Republican Congress dedicated to reducing taxes and cutting government spending. There was deep concern, not only in Congress but throughout the country, that scarce American goods would be drained off the domestic market for foreign consumption. There was similar concern lest the United States strain its financial and material resources only to 'pour its money down a rat hole,' and it was asked whether success of the program would serve only to increase competition for American business." [17]

These were serious questions that had to be carefully answered by the proponents of the Plan. Commenting on the work of the administration, Vandenberg wrote, "The preparations that the State Department has made for this next showdown are amazing. I have never seen better work. Indeed, they have simply overwhelmed us with documentation. I got the report of the Harriman Commission. . . . It is a magnificent piece of work." [18] Senator Vandenberg himself worked unstintingly to win support for the Marshall Plan; he was an avid letter writer, and much of his correspondence was in behalf of this program. A letter to Clark M. Eichelberger, Director of the American Association for the United Nations, demonstrated the importance attributed to the role of public opinion by a skillful strategist. "I have no illusions about this so-called 'Marshall Plan'," Vandenberg advised Eichelberger. "Furthermore, I certainly do not take it for granted that American public opinion is ready for any such burdens as would be involved unless and until it is far more effectively demonstrated to the American people that this (1) is within the latitudes of their own available resources and (2) serves their own intelligent self-interest." [19]

In the *Washington Post* the Alsops also emphasized the challenge that confronted the administration. An unidentified Senator is quoted as saying that "if Bevin and Bidault and the Europeans came up with a first-rate plan tomorrow and Marshall asked for the necessary appropriations the day after, he'd be turned down flat by an overwhelming majority in both Houses." [20]

As the legislative struggle over the Marshall Plan began, it was difficult to predict the final outcome. The fact that the Republicans controlled the Congress and the Democrats the administration was but one obstacle. The hearings of the Senate Foreign Relations Committee were so prolonged that it was said of Senator Vandenberg that he was trying to kill "the opposition to the Marshall Plan with kindness."

As more and more citizens became aware of the importance of the legislation, leaders of the administration and members of the State Department talked with as many different groups as possible throughout the country. Finally, to generate more public discussion, the creation of a special citizen's Committee for the Marshall Plan was announced on November 17, 1947. Credit has often been given to Henry L. Stimson for providing the incentive in an article in the October 1947 issue of *Foreign Affairs* entitled "The Challenge to Americans" which concluded with the following statement: "How soon this nation will fully understand the size and nature of its present mission, I do not dare to say. But I venture to assert that in very large degree the future of mankind depends on the answer to this question. And I am confident that if the issues are clearly presented, the American people will give the right answer. Surely there is here a fair and tempting challenge to all Americans, and especially to the nation's leaders, in and out of office." [21]

After this expression of faith in the ultimate wisdom of an informed public, Stimson was offered and accepted the national chairmanship of the Committee. More than three hundred other eminent Americans joined in this effort, and Robert P. Patterson became chairman of the Executive Committee. The aims of the group were summarized in a report: "The Committee is distributing printed material, arranging for speakers, and working with other existing organizations for an increasing attention to the Marshall Plan and support of its legitimate objectives. A petition to the Congress is being circulated calling for legislation to provide a sound and adequate program, in light of Secretary Marshall's proposal to aid European Recovery." [22]

Within two months, a campaign director's report stated, the Committee was able to distribute 375,000 pieces of literature. There was actually a greater demand for printed material than could be met. The relationship between this private Committee and the Department of State is a particularly interesting one. The Department of State, which had prepared an elaborate pamphlet on the Marshall Plan, had been under fire from Congress for the alleged use of "propaganda." When it was decided, therefore, that the Department could not print the pamphlet, the manuscript was offered to the Committee, for printing under its auspices. [23]

All of the intensive work done by the government, the bipartisan backing in the Congress, as well as the work by private organizations and leading citizens, generated strong public support for the program. The Marshall Plan was approved by the Congress ten months after Secretary of State Marshall had presented his original proposal. [24] The bill was passed by a large majority, 329 to 74, in the House on March 31, 1948; and there were only 17 votes against the bill in the Senate.

Given the extensive public debate of this subject, it is very likely that the Congress would have approved the program even if the country had not been enveloped in an atmosphere of crisis during March and April of 1948. The primary cause for this mood was the Communist *coup d'état* in Czechoslovakia on February 24, 1948. The vehement Communist opposition to the European Recovery Program, the Communist-led strikes (particularly in France and Italy at the turn of the year), and the pending Italian elections which we feared the Communists might win, all contributed to the tension.

President Truman delivered two speeches on foreign policy just prior to the vote in Congress on the Marshall Plan, in which he addressed himself more firmly to the problem of Russian intransigence than he had heretofore. To a joint session of Congress on March 17, 1948, Truman spoke of our responsibility to the Western world to prevent further Communist encroachment. He called for sufficient strength so that we would be able "to support those countries of Europe which are threatened with Communist control and police-state rule." As the editor of the Forrestal diary points out, this was "the first time the President identified the Soviet Union as the one nation that was blocking all efforts toward the writing of a peace and was aggressively threatening the free world." [25] Interestingly, the President not only utilized this opportunity to call for speedy action on the European Recovery Program, but he also recommended "prompt enactment of universal training legislation" as well as "the temporary re-enactment of selective service legislation." [26]

The events in Czechoslovakia had given a new urgency to the question of universal military training. Forrestal reports that Senator Saltonstall, a member of the Armed Services Committee, had stressed that "it would be impossible for the Senate to make any progress" unless Secretary Marshall and presumably other leaders of the administration could convince the country that there was a close relationship between universal military training and the conduct of our foreign policy. [27]

Seemingly without hesitation, the President interjected the highly controversial issues of universal training and selective service legislation into his appeals for support of the European Recovery Program. The introduction of these two issues so soon before the dramatic vote on the Marshall Plan might easily have weakened Truman's public support, yet again he operated on the assumption that frank and open presentation of the facts would win him public approval.

These two historic programs of the Truman administration emphasize the role of executive leadership in winning support for the administration's policies. One wonders whether it is possible for any administration or President to explain all its policies in such a way as to win consistent public backing. Certainly this was not possible in the Truman administration, despite the admirable work that was done and the President's firm belief in the rational attitude of public opinion. Our China policy was never clearly explained, probably because it was not clearly determined. Long before the Truman administration, as well as after it, the American people were unable to distinguish between fact and myth in Far Eastern affairs.

According to President Truman, the most significant act of his administration was the decision to resist aggression in Korea. This, however, falls into a completely different category of decision-making because of the extremely limited time-span during which the action had to be taken. Recent research has clearly established that the determination to enter the Korean war was strictly an executive decision based, as Rostow has pointed out, on the broad general and symbolic considerations involved—not necessarily the strategic value of the area.[28] Though we may note that two important bipartisan meetings did take place with Congressional leaders, these meetings served primarily to inform the participants about steps that had already been taken.

In light of the subsequent public criticism of American operations in Korea, the lack of Congressional approval of our original intervention has been questioned. Professor Glenn D. Paige makes the following comment based on an interview with Secretary of State Acheson: "With the morale of the American combat forces in mind, the Secretary of State did not want to risk exposing the decisions to possible attacks by legislators such as Republican Senator William E. Jenner of Indiana. He also did not want to precipitate a general discussion of the ultimate costs or consequences of military intervention in the Korean fighting." [29]

This, however, concerns the means by which the action was to be carried out, not the basic executive decision of whether we would support military intervention. Professor Paige reminds us that, although today American intervention may be seen as inevitable, "there is also ample evidence that observers in Washington were predicting on Monday, June 26, 1950, that the United States would not undertake direct military intervention in Korea at the very time that such a decision was being taken." [30]

A study of the military intervention in Korea is not within our scope. Korea has been cited merely as an illustration of a situation which required an almost instantaneous presidential decision. Despite the many advisors who were at the Chief Executive's elbow during the crucial week of June 24-30, 1950, the loneliness and responsibility of the ultimate decision-maker is classically illustrated here.

The first formal radio broadcast after the attack, in which the President explained our involvement in Korea, was not scheduled until July 19, 1950; and his second public broadcast did not take place until September 1, 1950. In the first broadcast the President described the events that led up to our involvement, and in the second he tried to explain the significance of the conflict to the individual American. Subsequently, we know, the administration failed to communicate adequately the aims and goals of this struggle. While American objectives in Korea, or for that matter in the Cuban crisis, or in South Viet Nam, were or are relatively easy to explain, it is not easy to make clear the complex decisions which have to be made or to rationalize the limitations on our ability to make certain decisions. Repeatedly, in one postwar crisis after another, Presidents have experienced great difficulty in explaining and defending the intricate and limited means employed to achieve oversimplified objectives. Americans, for example, could understand and approve the following statement made by the President in his radio address of September 1, 1950. "If the history of the 1930's teaches us anything it is that appeasement of dictators is the sure road to world war. If aggression were allowed to succeed in Korea, it would be an open invitation to new acts of aggression elsewhere."

Afterward, the citizen asks questions about costs and time and demands concrete evidence that the general goal is being achieved; when he observes that the full military power of the United States is not being employed to win "victory," he becomes dissatisfied and frustrated. These negative emotions easily breed mounting dissensions and suspicions. At such a time, all the tools of presidential leadership seem incapable of stemming the tide of criticism. It is then that the destiny of the nation is tied most closely to the vision and courage of the Chief Executive—a man who must be able to foresee the future, who must have a sense of history, and who must understand the times in which he lives.[31]

CHAPTER XIV

CONTRASTS AND COMPARISONS

We have attempted to determine how two Presidents assessed and aroused public opinion in the formulation of foreign policy during two climactic periods in recent American history. Though decision-making is unquestionably multifaceted, we have concentrated on the executive-public relationship. This has the danger of overemphasizing one facet, yet it has the advantage of providing clearer insights into a major aspect of the decision-making processs.

A former Secretary of State, Christian A. Herter, has said: "A successful foreign policy must, . . . to be effective, command the support of the vast majority of the American people—otherwise it would not be given the tools by the Congress which are essential to its fulfillment."[1] Foster observes that "a broad public understanding greatly aids the government as it develops new policies to meet new conditions."[2] These statements aptly summarize many questions considered in this book. How is the action of a President affected by the presence of or lack of broad public understanding? How does he measure, evaluate, and foster public support? During both periods under consideration, the interests of the United States were challenged by a strong power representing an alien ideology. During both periods, many citizens did not recognize that the challenge required a more positive foreign policy.

A study of the relationship between the Chief Executive and the public is difficult to analyze and frustrating to evaluate because of its inherent intangibility. Since motivations and attitudes are involved, we are restricted in our sources and, as one writer has emphasized, are forced "to rely on whatever observations journalists, government officials, and others may have recorded at the time, and on the subsequent recollections of people who participated in the event."[3] In the opinion of E. Malcolm Carroll "the value of a study of public opinion does not mainly depend upon its immediate influence upon the ruler's decisions. How the public reacted and why are, to my mind, interesting and significant questions for their own sake."[4] We can attempt to evaluate all of the influences, including the role of public opinion, which impelled Presidents Roosevelt and Truman to act as they did; but at best the scholar can only partially recreate

102

the multiple forces which influenced the decisions of a Chief Executive.

Theoretical formulations (beyond the one that it is easier to pursue a particular foreign policy with public support than without it) are extremely difficult considering the great number of fluctuating circumstances involving human behavior and institutions, all influenced by the social, political, and economic forces of a fluid and dramatic period. Comparative study is particularly useful, however, because it permits effective differential analysis of leadership techniques employed in specific situations, not withstanding such major changes as the weakening of isolationist fervor, disparate personalities, or institutional changes affecting one branch of the government or the relations between different branches.

The differences in the approaches of Presidents Roosevelt and Truman in seeking public support for precedent-setting policies were the result of differences in personality as well as in the circumstances in which these innovations were formulated. Truman's frankness and readiness to tackle foreign policy issues served him well in the political climate of the post-1945 era. These very same characteristics, however, could not have been utilized as effectively in the pre-World War II period. It is probable that Truman's occasional impatience and his readiness to engage in public battle would have lent encouragement to the isolationist opposition if exercised in the immediate prewar years.

Under President Truman, the administration deliberately, step-by-step, planted the seeds it expected to flower into public understanding and support for a number of innovations in American foreign policy that required legislative approval. Information and the rationale for new programs were supplied by the administration, Congress, and private organizations. A special appeal for support was directed to such elite groups as businessmen, editors, religious leaders, and Congressmen. The President is in the key position to direct such a broad program of persuasion and education. Truman himself reinforced these appeals by informal meetings with selected leaders, by press conferences, and by occasional speeches and official announcements.

President Truman's responsibility for gaining acceptance of his policies was simplified by the fact that, during his first administration, he was not as controversial as President Roosevelt had been. He also worked more closely and effectively with his staff (particularly his Secretaries of State Marshall and Acheson) than Roosevelt did. This meant that, in the invariable confrontations with the Congress, President Truman was not always in the limelight. To a degree this can enhance the posture and flexibility of a President because some influence is left in reserve to be utilized at the most propitious moment to win crucial votes in the Congress or to make a final appeal to the public for support. President Roosevelt, looming so much larger and being less dependent on his subordinates, sometimes had to resort to silence in order to deemphasize his role with regard to policies for which he sought public support and legislative sanction.

Both Presidents were highly conscious of the importance of the necessary preparatory work, so that the general public and the Congress would accept the President's legislative program. The record indicates that Roosevelt was always wary of his political opposition. Concerned with leading opinion, he modulated his position according to the pace of his followers. As important as these political manipulations were for the purpose of attaining legislative victories, our study demonstrates that Roosevelt's lack of frankness profoundly disturbed some of his advisors and supporters. The deliberate blurring of issues to gain political advantage in the legislature made it more difficult to gain public confidence.

President Truman's attitude toward Congress can best be shown by an anecdote related by William S. White. As a part of a carefully planned and intensive effort to win support for the Greek and Turkish aid program, President Truman invited Congressional delegations to the White House for discussion. In these sessions Truman outlined what he intended to do and asked for comments. "One of the Congressional deputations would ask, 'But what, Mr. President, what of the political implications to the party of all this?' Truman would turn in cold anger upon him and say slowly, 'In these matters I never want to hear that damn word politics mentioned here again.' "[5]

Bipartisan techniques in the formulation of foreign policy were utilized more effectively during the Truman administration than under Roosevelt. The circumstances, of course, were quite different. The 80th Congress which met on January 3, 1947, consisted of 51 Republicans and 45 Democrats in the Senate and 244 Republicans and 188 Democrats in the House. Much credit for the success of the bipartisan approach must go to Senator Arthur H. Vandenberg (Republican of Michigan), who was the chairman of the Senate Foreign Relations Committee. Bipartisanship under Roosevelt was exemplified by appointment of two well-known Republicans (Knox and Stimson) to the Cabinet, his efforts to maintain cordial relations with Wendell Willkie after the 1940 elections, and his close association with the

Republican editor, William Allen White. These efforts were disappointing. The resentments aroused by his startling appointments to the Cabinet hindered the unity he desired. The inadequacy of the appointment of one lone nonpolitical Republican (Henry White) to President Wilson's executive delegation to the Paris Peace Conference comes readily to mind.

President Truman, once the "right" course was determined, rarely vacillated. Only for a very short period did he continue the efforts of the previous administration to win the trust and confidence of the Soviet leaders. Events soon made it absolutely clear that the United States would adopt a policy of firmness. There is no evidence that the President was ever troubled by self-doubt about the direction followed by his administration. Some segments of the population were confused by the rapid turn of events leading to a hardening of positions between the United States and the Soviet Union, and they questioned the legitimacy of our response. The threat to American security, however, was quickly seen through what was at first a mist of frustration and doubt as the hopes for peace, disarmament, and the effectiveness of the United Nations as a peace-keeping instrument disintegrated. It is doubtful that the administration could have as quickly achieved public and Congressional support for its new policy of firmness if the nation had not been afraid of communism. Ideological issues now played a much more significant role than in the period before the Second World War. The American people were willing to accept the fact that the Communist ideology represented a greater threat to their personal well-being than Fascism. And it was the public's emphasis on the ideological confrontation after 1945 which quickly intensified the demand for firmness in the face of threatened Soviet expansionism. We would be doing the public an injustice, however, to assume that support for the administration's policy was based solely on a fear of communism. In the main, Americans appreciated the fact that new responsibilities had fallen on us; our range of interests had widened and, as Dexter Perkins has noted, "sensitiveness to aggression [had] meritedly increased."[9]

Sumner Welles offers a partial explanation for President Roosevelt's reluctance to issue forthright public appeals prior to Pearl Harbor for a policy of assistance and firmness in support of the anti-Nazi coalition. Welles observes that, while the President did not have a "one-track mind," he preferred "to segregate the urgent from the not-so-urgent." He was inclined "to devote himself to the task which was immediate rather than to the task which could be undertaken later on."[7] Accepting, therefore, the state of negative public opinion toward the dangers of involvement in a war and fearing a political set-back on any one of the several important measures he wanted approved by the Congress, the President set his sights on getting each required legislative item approved one by one. As a policy-maker, he was convinced that "policy had to stay within the bounds of toleration set by opinion."[8]

Nothing here should imply that the President did not appreciate the significance of a German victory. As a matter of fact, he understood the impact of such a catastrophe better than most. The problem which confronted him was chiefly one of when to make assistance available to the Allies. In his reluctance to spell out publicly the implications of an Axis victory (although he certainly did this often before selected groups), he was simply reinforcing the position of a small but troublesome disaffected minority which might have been influential in preventing American involvement. The evidence indicates that, if the President had been convinced that it was possible to encourage a shift of opinion to support of what the administration wanted to do, he would have exercised more vigorous public leadership in marshaling and channeling this opinion. In the final analysis, President Roosevelt's success or failure in dealing with public opinion on foreign policy cannot be fully measured because the attack against Pearl Harbor automatically generated complete public support.

Our study has demonstrated that, up to the rejection of the Quarantine Address, the President made a concerted effort to lead public opinion. It would be useless to speculate about what policies the President might have pursued if the Quarantine Address had not been received so critically. In the President's estimation, the element of time must have been crucial. Was there time to educate the public, or was there only enough time for a concerted effort to fight for the minimum legislation which would prepare the country for the eventual dangers it faced?

Why did Roosevelt make the choice he did?

The President had become overly sensitive to negative public opinion and had overestimated the influence of the isolationists. I think the record indicates that the President allowed the vociferous isolationist pressure groups and the results of the polls to limit the educative role inherent in the office of the Chief Executive. The result, as we have seen, was that the demands of other opinion-elites for leadership and guidance were submerged, not alone in the context of the times, but also in the subsequent literature, in which it has received scant attention.

Congress also presented formidable opposition to administration policy. President Roosevelt assumed a close relationship between Congressional views and public opinion. Comparison of the polls with Congressional attitudes indicates that, on a number of important issues, such as the elimination of the Neutrality Act and conscription, the people were favorably inclined before the Congress reluctantly took action. Not infrequently Congress has lagged behind public opinion. Elmer Davis has commented that "Congress is usually an accurate barometer of public opinion only when that opinion is so unmistakable that no barometer is needed."[9] In the final analysis, however, it is almost impossible for the Chief Executive to promote a consensus in support of a policy if he cannot count on the Congress for a dispassionate and frank consideration of the issues.[10]

President Roosevelt's total sympathy for the Allied powers and his conviction that the physical security of the United States was at stake needs no further documentation. One may speculate that the President assumed that the events overseas and various incidents directly involving the United States, such as the sinking of the Athenia, accompanied by direct administration action could, to some degree, "elicit the pressures which [would] propel him along the course he already [had] chosen to go."[11]

The President must have been dismayed to discover that the American public was not aware that they had a direct and tangible stake in the outcome of the struggle overseas. The only alternative was to seek the necessary legislation from Congress without strengthening the revulsion to any action which might lead to American involvement. Only with vain hindsight then, may any observer suggest that the President should have taken a firmer stand in winning public support for the legislation which he was trying to push through Congress and for the administrative decisions which he made by fiat.

We may note that the President was keenly aware that "political leadership almost always involves an ingredient of followership."[12] He may have been overconsciously aware of it, not in terms of the action which he pursued, but in the way he communicated with the American people.

Why was Roosevelt's method of handling a difficult situation so different from the rational and less complicated approach of Harry S. Truman? Because a number of significant changes had occurred in the outlook of the American public, President Truman's appeals for a

firm and constructive foreign policy gained a more positive response
than those of President Roosevelt. By 1946 Americans not only recognized the aggressive and expanding power of the Soviet Union, but
they also acknowledged the need for a policy of firmness and responsibility to preserve the security of the non-communist world.

We should reemphasize at this point that, despite their differing
attitudes toward the role of public opinion, neither President Roosevelt nor President Truman underestimated its influence. Each, however, utilized his understanding in a different way. President Roosevelt primarily worked to win some key legislative struggles and hoped
to arouse public sympathy for his objectives. In contrast, President
Truman carefully planned public information programs which would
gain the understanding and public support without which it is difficult to win any legislative struggle. It is clear, however, that even
when enlightened support of public opinion is available, the need for
political leadership is not diminished; with public support for a national policy, however, the road toward the successful approval and
application of a legislative policy will be much less rocky.

Timing may be the crucial factor in determining when the President
should utilize his considerable powers of public persuasion. Since
President Roosevelt appreciated this point, he never openly supported
the interventionist position, in the fear of the overwhelming protests
that would ensue. In the Truman administration, information regarding the climate of public opinion regulated the coordination of public
education with policy formulation in an effort to push legislation
through the Congress.

In our democratic system, political manipulation which dispenses
with the support and sympathy of the public is not the best way to
promote legislation. It is politically unhealthy for the Chief Executive
attempting it; and it may on occasion lead to political suicide. Today,
greater public sophistication and improved modes of communication
require the President, with courage and conviction, to make much
information available in connection with policies that the administration wishes to pursue.

We may make two primary observations on presidential leadership
during periods of crisis. First, the arduous task of policy formulation
is eased considerably when a President is not visibly troubled by self-
doubt or indecision in regard to the policies to be pursued and the
ultimate goals to be achieved. Second, the task of gaining public support is eased when the public is emotionally involved and is convinced
that the policy and goals are commensurate with the potential risks.

When an administration is confronted with doubts, confusion, or apathy about the national interest, as was the case before World War II, obfuscation is no solution. Our two case studies demonstrate the importance of candor in clearly spelling out policy alternatives without propagandizing. An administration must be willing to stake its prestige and its political survival on a particular course of action without sacrificing the indispensable quality of flexibility.

That these observations are not as elementary as they seem is exemplified by the fact that President Roosevelt—to a lesser degree, President Truman—and other Presidents who succeeded them have indulged in sloganeering and ambiguity to the detriment of their policies. Why? The reasons, though not always clear, stem partly from a lack of confidence in the ability of the public to distinguish primary from secondary goals; partly from an inability to focus clearly and efficiently on what the public needs or wants to know; and partly from the necessity of considering the impact on other nations of statements directed to the American people. The Korean war and the struggle in Southeast Asia are cases in point.

The public cannot be asked to voice constructive opinions if the leadership has not provided it with adequate and honest information. James N. Rosenau has pointed out that in recent years we have expected too much from strong Presidential leadership. He suggests that, if basic differences really exist among different segments of the public, it is likely that "even the most vigorous of Presidents is bound to be a less than successful consensus-builder."[13] This warning does not, however, have direct applicability to this work since we have been primarily concerned with general problems which clearly had a national impact. In a genuine crisis it remains the responsibility of the President to nationalize the issues.

Professor Lasswell wrote some years ago that the public judges issues on the basis of symbols or their symbolic significance. More recently another scholar, reflecting on the role of leadership in the contemporary world, wrote, "And what symbol can be more reassuring than the incumbent of a high position who knows what to do and is willing to act, especially when others are bewildered and alone."[14]

Lasswell emphasizes that "the mass public does not study and analyze detailed data" on a wide variety of public issues. It ignores the issues "until political actions and speeches make them symbolically threatening or reassuring, and it then responds to the cues furnished by the actions and the speeches, not to direct knowledge of the facts."[15] Dealing more directly with the realities of this problem, Dean Rusk wrote: "What the American people will do turns in large degree on their leadership. We cannot test public opinion until the President and the leaders of the country have gone to the public to explain what is required and have asked them for support for the necessary action. I doubt, for example, that, 3 months before the leadership began to talk about what came to be the Marshall Plan, any public opinion expert would have said that the country would have accepted such proposals."[16]

Before our involvement in the Second World War, a number of symbols were prized by those Americans who believed that we had to stay out of the conflict at all cost. The fear of socialism and the emphasis on the need to uphold the doctrine of isolationism had symbolic significance because these ideas represented fears of greater evils that could befall us if America became involved in another war. To most people immediate and personal threats became a symbol for fears which actually extended over a wider periphery.

Similarly, communism had symbolic significance after 1945. The specter of a hated ideology facilitated the pursuit of important innovations in American foreign policy during peacetime. A specific occurrence, such as the *coup d'état* in Prague in February 1948, was such a striking illustration of Russian policy that this single event assumed an aura of symbolic significance and generated public support for the inauguration of historic new policies in support of the containment doctrine.

Democratic government can only function successfully if there is a reciprocal faith between leaders and followers. The historian Ernest R. May believes that the chief reason for the influence of public opinion on foreign policy is our knowledge that "American statesmen have traditionally thought themselves responsible to, and supported or constrained by, some sort of general will."[17] The President, particularly with respect to foreign policy, indicates his faith in democracy by taking the people into his confidence. If he falters in his faith, resorts to cynicism, or begins to feel omnipotent, he assumes that the people are no longer capable of judging policy or of choosing from the given alternatives the policy which represents the nation's best interests. Our study of the relationship between public opinion and leadership indicates that Presidents Roosevelt and Truman retained their faith in the "common man"[18] to a remarkable degree, although President Roosevelt certainly experienced a crisis of confidence.

The nature of the relationship between leadership and followership in the making of foreign policy has long challenged the political theorist and practitioner alike. The concept of leadership in a democratic society must become more meaningful in the light of the changing realities of every generation. Beyond this, there is no ultimate solution but the recognition that democratic government will only retain its vitality if we recognize "that leaders and the led provide essential psychological benefits for each other."[19]

An important factor differentiates more recent foreign policy crises (e.g., Berlin, Korea, Cuba, South Vietnam) from the ones examined in this study. In these latter-day crises, I believe the role of public opinion has been much less significant in policy formulation than it had been previously. Certainly, since the 1939-1941 period, foreign policy decisions, particularly those involving crisis situations, have become much more technical and more closely related to bedrock national security issues than before. The explanation is not solely the impact of the technological changes in the military realm, but also the ideological confrontation of the different Powers. This global competition involves techniques ranging from propaganda and economic warfare to military assistance which now has been stretched to include limited war.

Most postwar crises have arisen suddenly, which in turn means that the use of governmental machinery to deal with them has been maximized. *Ad hoc* organs are set up for specific situations. These procedures have minimized the influence of public opinion on the decision-making process. Time has been of the essence. Government has been so busy digesting essential information that there has been little time to relay it effectively to the public. This in itself has precluded a rational and constructive formulation of public opinion at the time of the crisis; the public cannot really react to sudden threat except in an emotional way.

A prolonged confrontation raises doubts and frustrations regarding inadequate or overextended commitments. For this reason it becomes especially important that the administration strive to make accurate information available, issue forthright statements, attempt to promote confidence. The President should personally utilize the prestige of his office to seek understanding and support in preparation for the time when the public begins to question the nature of the struggle or the response to a challenge facing the nation.

The whole structure of executive leadership in contemporary America has become increasingly complex. In such crises as Korea, Cuba, and the Gulf of Tonkin the President headed a decision-making apparatus. Executive policy formulation has become a more intricate organizational process, although the President himself still retains ultimate responsibility. Only after an immediate response has been decided upon can the administration work to win support and trust for a long-range policy. Sometimes, the President may request public acknowledgement of support at the time of the crisis. This show of unity may serve a more important function externally than internally, because internally the long-run position of public opinion is more important than the immediate response. A noteworthy example was the rapidity with which the Congressional Resolution was approved supporting American foreign policy in Southeast Asia after American warships were reported to have been attacked in the Gulf of Tonkin. This resolution, as others before it,[20] gave the President a remarkably free hand to deal with a large variety of situations that might arise. Despite considerable prior skepticism and criticism regarding American foreign policy in Southeast Asia, this resolution was approved by a vote of 416-0 after a forty-minute debate in the House of Representatives and 88-2 in the Senate after a nine-hour debate. Thus, the President can win immediate and overwhelming bipartisan support with little effort when sudden and frightening crisis threatens American interests.[21]

On the other hand, there may be areas of equal importance, but not so obviously critical, for which the leadership cannot generate support. Chief Executives have stressed to the public the importance of foreign aid as an instrument of American foreign policy. Nevertheless, the appropriations have been cut; and, even more significantly, the authority of the Chief Executive to utilize this aid as he sees fit has been circumscribed.

We can only conclude that, no matter how able and foresighted the President may be, his talent to lead depends to some extent upon the circumstances and the environment in which he operates. From time to time, though, the republic will be blessed with a great leader who possesses a special ability to win the support and sympathy of the people for the policies he wishes to pursue. But such men are rare in a nation's history. Dean Acheson has observed that "in our American system the President is the person charged with the heavy duty of giving us the line to follow in our dealings with other nations."[22] This is certainly the minimum we expect from our Chief Executive, and he cannot escape this responsibility.

There is really only one proved method for sound and effective leadership. Churchill spoke the following words during time of war, but they are as applicable today as when he said them: "Nothing is more dangerous than to live in the temperamental atmosphere of a Gallup poll, always feeling one's pulse and taking one's temperature . . . There is only one duty, only one safe course, and that is to try to be right and not to fear to do or say what you belive to be right." This above all must be the key to the relationship between the Chief Executive and the citizens of the land.

REFERENCES

CHAPTER I

1 See discussion of this issue in Gabriel A. Almond, *The American People and Foreign Policy* (New York: Harcourt, Brace and Company, 1950), pp. 5-6. "The function of the public in a democratic policymaking process is to set certain policy criteria in the form of widely held values and expectations. It evaluates the results of policies from the point of their conformity to these basic values and expectations. The policies themselves, however, are the products of leadership groups ["elites"] who carry on the specific work of policy formulation and advocacy."

2 Hans J. Morgenthau, *The Purpose of American Politics* (New York: Alfred A. Knopf, 1960), p. 262.

3 "It is plain that elections involve broad decisions on policy questions, although estimation of precisely what those determinations are requires a degree of artistry." V. O. Key, Jr., *Public Opinion and American Democracy* (New York: Alfred A. Knoplf, 1960), p. 478.

4 Robert A. Dahl, *A Preface to Democratic Theory* (Chicago: University of Chicago Press, 1956), p. 130.

5 Dexter Perkins, "Foreign Policy in Presidential Campaigns," *Foreign Affairs,* Vol. 35, No. 2 (January, 1957), p. 216.

6 *Ibid.,* p. 224.

7 Angus Campbell, Philip Converse, Warren E. Miller, and Donald Stokes, *The American Voter* (New York: Wiley, 1960).

8 Murray Edelman, review of *The American Voter,* in *Midwest Journal of Political Science,* Vol. V, No. 1 (February, 1961), p. 85. See also the challenging essay by Herbert McClosky, "Consensus and Ideology in American Politics," *The American Political Science Review* (APSR), Vol. LVIII, No. 2 (June, 1964), pp. 378-79.

9 *Ibid.*

10 V. O. Key, Jr., "Public Opinion and the Decay of Democracy," *The Virginia Quarterly Review,* Vol. 37, No. 4 (Autumn, 1961), p. 487. Key states that the only occasion on which the voters give a clear indication of their preferences is when they express dissatisfaction with past policy or performance by not returning public officials to office. See also Key, Jr., *Public Opinion and American Democracy,* p. 473.

11 *The Rockefeller Panel Reports,* "Prospects for America" (Garden City, New York: Doubleday, 1961), p. 78.

[Roger Hilsman notes an important qualification when he states that "There are limits to how far one can go in bringing the general population into the details of policy-making. If so, the essence of democracy may be not so much that the people perform the daily tasks of government by choosing between policies as that the goals of the people are served. Thus in a diverse, mass society, democracy might be better served by efforts at improving the rationality and effectiveness of the process by which values are identified, weighted, and reconciled, including the place of elections in this, and by insuring that the process is an open one, accessible to anyone who is interested . . ." "The Foreign-Policy Consensus: An

Interim Research Report," *Journal of Conflict Resolution*, Vol. 3, No. 4 (1959), pp. 380-81.]

12 Gabriel A. Almond, *The American People and Foreign Policy, op. cit.*, pp. 139-141. Almond categorizes political, administrative or bureaucratic, interest, and communications elites. Given the complexity of foreign affairs and the inapplicability of some foreign policy issues, even these elite groups may react with indifference to some issues.

13 *Ibid.*, p. 138. The "attentive public" is invariably interested in foreign affairs. The term "general public" refers to those who are easily buffeted about by the torrent of news concerning foreign affairs, or are completely uninformed. See the most recent categorizations by James N. Rosenau, *Public Opinion and Foreign Policy* (New York: Random House, 1961), Chapter 3. Analyzing the relationship between public opinion and foreign policy he distinguishes three different but related processes: the governmental decision-making process, the opinion-submitting process, and the opinion-making process.

14 James N. Rosenau, *Public Opinion and Foreign Policy, op. cit.*, Chapter 5, 15 *Ibid.*, p. 72.

16 Henry M. Wriston, *Diplomacy in a Democracy* (New York: Harper & Brothers, 1956), p. 40.

17 Quincy Wright, "The Importance of The Study of International Tensions," *International Social Science Bulletin*, Vol. II, No. 1 (Spring, 1950), p. 99.

18 Recent studies dealing with different facets of the Presidency include the following books: *The President's Cabinet* (1959) by Richard F. Fenno, Jr.; *The Ultimate Decision: The President as Commander-in-Chief* (1960) by Ernest R. May (ed.); *Presidential Power: The Politics of Leadership* (1960) by Richard E. Neustadt; *The Presidency and Individual Liberties* (1961) by Richard P. Longaker; *Presidential Leadership of Public Opinion* (1965) by Elmer E. Cornwell, Jr.

19 Quoted in Bernard R. Berelson, Paul F. Lazarsfeld, William N. McPhee, *Voting* (Chicago: The University of Chicago Press, 1954), p. 305.

20 *Ibid.*, p. 309.

21 Quoted in Berelson, *Ibid.*, p. 307.

22 Gabriel A. Almond, *The American People and Foreign Policy, op. cit.*, pp. 5-6, 138. Also Lester Markel (ed.) *Public Opinion and Foreign Policy* (New York: Harper & Brothers, 1949).

23 Robert A. Nisbet, "The Study of Man: Voting Practices vs. Democratic Theory," *Commentary*, Vol. 31, No. 1 (January, 1961), p. 64.

24 *Ibid.*, p. 65.

25 Quoted in Berelson, *op. cit.*, p. 312.

26 Edward A. Shils, *The Torment of Secrecy* (Glencoe, Illinois: The Free Press, 1956), p. 21.

27 Key, Jr., *The Virginia Quarterly Review, op. cit.*, p. 489-491.

28 Charles Burton Marshall, *The Limits of Foreign Policy* (New York: Henry Holt and Co., 1954), p. 13.

29 Lester B. Pearson, *Democracy in World Politics* (Princeton, New Jersey: Princeton University Press, 1955), p. 107.

30 Arthur Schlesinger, Jr., Book review of *Public Opinion, 1935-1946*, in *The Public Opinion Quarterly*, Vol. 15, No. 1 (Spring, 1951), p. 149.

31 W. W. Rostow, *The United States in the World Arena* (New York: Harper & Brothers, 1960), p. 511.

32 Key, Jr., *The Virginia Quarterly Review, op. cit.,* p. 486.

33 *Ibid.,* p. 488.

34 Harold Lasswell, *Democracy Through Public Opinion* (George Banta Publishing Company, 1941), p. 15, 18.

35 Hans J. Morgenthau, *In Defense of the National Interests: A Critical Examination of Foreign Policy* (New York: Alfred A. Knopf, 1951), p. 228. [This distinction between what the leadership thinks it ought to do and what it thinks it can do in a democracy has been widely discussed in the literature. See for example Louis J. Halle, *Dreams and Reality: Aspects of American Foreign Policy* (New York: Harper, 1959), pp. 304-309; Max Beloff, *Foreign Policy and the Democratic Process* (Baltimore: The Johns Hopkins Press, 1955).]

36 Walter Lippmann, *The Public Philosophy* (New York: Mentor Book, 1955), p. 46. See also *The Phantom Public* (New York: Harcourt, Brace and Company, 1925), Chapters IV and XIII.

37 Lippmann, *The Public Philosophy,* pp. 23-24.

38 A. L. Rowse, *The End of an Epoch* (London: Macmillan & Co., Ltd., 1948), p. 94.

39 A. L. Rowse, *Appeasement: A Study in Political Decline, 1933-1939* (New York: W. W. Norton & Company, Inc., 1961), p. 58.

40 Schlesinger, Jr., *The Public Opinion Quarterly, op. cit.,* p. 149.

41 Cited in A. L. Rowse, *End of an Epoch, op. cit.,* p. 171.

42 Center for the Study of Democratic Institutions, *The Elite and The Electorate: Is Government by the People Possible?* (Santa Barbara, California: The Fund for the Republic, Inc., 1963). See essay by J. William Fulbright, p. 4.

43 *Ibid.,* p. 5.

CHAPTER II

1 James Aloysius Farley, *Jim Farley's Story* (New York: Whittlesey House, 1948), p. 56.

2 FDR, PPF 6011. Hamilton Fish Armstrong to F.D.R., February 15, 1934.

3 Others have reached a similar conclusion. Professor John P. Roche writes that "Whatever Roosevelt's inner convictions about Hitler may have been, his public statements of that period [the thirties] hardly indicated any great insight into the true dimensions of the Nazi menace." "Memo to Today's 'Young Radicals,'" *The New York Times Magazine,* October 14, 1962, p. 17.

4 Selig Adler, *The Isolationist Impulse: Its Twentieth Century Reaction* (New York: Collier Books, 1961), pp. 232-33.

5 Elliott Roosevelt (ed.), *Franklin Delano Roosevelt: His Personal Letters* (4 Vols., New York: Duell, Sloan, & Pearce, 1947-1950), 1928-1945, Vol. 3, F.D.R. to Colonel House, April 10, 1935, p. 472.

6 *Ibid.*

7 Elliott Roosevelt (ed.), *op. cit.,* (1928-1945), Vol. 3, pp. 472-73.

8 *Ibid.,* F.D.R. to Colonel House, September 17, 1935, pp. 506-507.

9 Willard Range, *Franklin D. Roosevelt's World Order* (Athens: University of Georgia Press, 1959), pp. x-xi.

10 Arthur M. Schlesinger, Jr., *The Age of Roosevelt: The Politics of Upheaval*, Vol. III (Boston: Houghton Mifflin Company, 1960), p. 263.

11 William L. Langer and S. Everett Gleason, *The Challenge to Isolation, 1937-1940* (New York: Harper & Brothers, 1952), p. 16.

12 Basil Rauch (ed.), *The Roosevelt Reader* (New York: Rinehart & Co., Inc., 1957), p. 145. Hereafter cited as Rauch (ed.).

13 Arthur M. Schlesinger, Jr., *op. cit.*, p. 502.

14 Basil Rauch, *Roosevelt: From Munich to Pearl Harbor; a study in the creation of a foreign policy* (New York: Creative Age Press, 1950), p. vii, 33. See also Cordell Hull, *The Memoirs of Cordell Hull*, Vol. 1 (New York: The Macmillan Company, 1948), pp. 479-480.

15 See accounts of Brussels Conference in Rauch, *Roosevelt: from Munich to Pearl Harbor, op. cit.*, pp. 49-52 and in Robert A. Divine's excellent study *The Illusion of Neutrality* (Chicago: The University of Chicago Press, 1962), pp. 213-14.

16 Anthony Eden, *The Memoirs of Anthony Eden: Facing the Dictators* (Boston: Houghton Mifflin Company, 1962), p. 610.

17 *Ibid.*, p. 616, quoting *The Memoirs of Cordell Hull*, Vol. I.

18 Langer and Gleason, *op. cit.*, p. 24, citing *Berliner Monatshefte*, February 1943, pp. 53-60.

19 Samuel I. Rosenman, *Working With Roosevelt* (New York: Harper & Brothers, 1952), p. 165.

20 Hull, *op. cit.*, p. 545. See also Rosenman, *op. cit.*, 165. Rosenman reports that Harold Ickes often talked to the President about matters not concerned with his Department, particularly about foreign affairs. He frequently criticized the weakness of the State Department. In one conversation with the President, Ickes referred to the international situation "as a disease, saying that a neighborhood has a right to 'quarantine' itself against a threatened infection." Apparently the President was interested in this analogy, noted the word, and commented that he might use it.

21 Rauch (ed.), *op. cit.*, pp. 187-92.

22 Franklin D. Roosevelt, *The Public Papers and Addresses of Franklin D. Roosevelt*, (Comp. by Samuel I. Rosenman), 1939, Vol. 8 (New York: The Macmillan Company, 1941), p. xxviii. Hereafter cited as Public Papers by year and volume.

23 The 1937 *Survey of International Affairs* said that "from the message to Congress on disarmament in 1934 down to the famous quarantine speech in Chicago at the end of 1937, the President and the Secretary of State literally set themselves the task of re-educating American opinion in the need for an active international policy." Quoted in Nicholas Halasz, *Roosevelt Through Foreign Eyes* (Princeton, New Jersey: Van Nostrand, 1961), p. 106. However, any attempt to re-educate the American public to support a more active policy in foreign affairs during this period was carried out in only a very general way.

24 Press Conference #400, Hyde Park, New York, October 6, 1937, pp. 2, 15-21.

25 FDR, PPF 200-B, Public Reaction Letters, Public Addresses, October 5, 1937, Boxes 82-84. Box 84, Mrs. H. Palen, Vineland, New Jersey to FDR, October 8, 1937.

26 *Ibid.*, Joseph Pointer to FDR, October 7, 1937. (Responses to this speech

fill three boxes; however, only a thin folder contains the letters which are critical of the President.)

27 *Ibid.*, F.D.R., PPF 200-B, Box 82.

28 *Ibid.*, Box 82.

29 Elliott Roosevelt (ed.), *op. cit.*, F.D.R. to Colonel House, October 19, 1937, p. 719.

30 Rauch (ed.), *op. cit.*, Letter to Rhoda Hinkley, December 16, 1937, pp. 192-93.

31 FDR, PPF 200-B, Box 83. Letter to James Roosevelt from Raymond Leslie Buell, President, Foreign Policy Association, October 20, 1937.

32 Hadley Cantril, "America Faces the War: A Study in Public Opinion," *The Public Opinion Quarterly*, Vol. 4, No. 3, September 1940, p. 405.

33 Nancy Boardman Eddy, *Public Opinion and United States Foreign Policy, 1937-1956*, American Project, Working Paper I, MIT, n.d., p. 14, citing AIPO.

34 Langer and Gleason, *op. cit.*, p. 38.

35 *Ibid.*, p. 39.

36 Donald F. Drummond, *The Passing of American Neutrality, 1937-1941* (Ann Arbor: The University of Michigan Press, 1955), p. 78.

37 *Ibid.*, p. 81.

38 Rauch, *Roosevelt: From Munich to Pearl Harbor, op. cit.*, p. 79.

39 Public Papers, *op. cit.*, 1939, Vol. 8, 523rd Press Conference, February 3, 1939, p. 115.

40 Conference 645-A. Conference with Members of the Business Advisory Council, Executive Office of the White House, May 23, 1940, p. 23.

CHAPTER III

1 Press Conference #518, Executive Offices of the White House, January 17, 1939.

2 This Committee was called in for an explanation of the crash of an American bomber with a French Air Ministry official on board.

3 Press Conference #525, on the President's Special Train en route from Washington to Florida City, Florida, February 17, 1939, 2:30 P.M., pp. 7-11.

4 Typical is the violent reaction to the suggestion by the President that he might have to return to Washington earlier than he had expected because "information that continues to be received with respect to the international situation continues to be disturbing. . . . It is understood that this information relates to the possible renewal of demands by certain countries, these demands being pushed, not through normal diplomatic channels but, rather, through more recent type of relations; in other words, the use of the fear of aggression." [The Germans marched into Czechoslovakia on March 15, 1937.] Press Conference #526, At the Civilian Conservation Corps Camp on West Summerfield Key, Florida, February 18, 1939, 12:45 P.M.

5 Rauch (ed.), *op. cit.*, p. 211.

6 Public Papers, 1939, Vol. 8, 523rd Press Conference, February 3, 1939, p. 110.

7 *Ibid.*, p. 111.

8 FDR, Group 13, PPF 1820, Box 24. From Clyde Eagleton to Dr. Stanley K.

Hornbeck, Political Advisor to State Department, February 16, 1939.

9 Press Conference #538, Executive Office of the White House, April 11, 1939, 4:00 P.M.

10 Robert E. Osgood, *Ideals and Self-Interest in America's Foreign Relations* (Chicago: The University of Chicago Press, 1953), p. 412.

11 FDR, Group 13, PPF, Box 24. Memorandum for the President, April 24, 1939, from A. A. Berle, Jr. [Berle was professor of corporation law at Columbia Law School and Assistant Secretary of State, 1938-1944.]

12 R. Walton Moore File, Library of Congress, December 27, 1939, Box 3. (Moore to Bullitt) [R. Walton Moore was elected to Congress, 1919-1931, appointed Assistant Secretary of State in 1933, and Counselor of the Department of State in 1937.]

13 Josephus Daniels Papers, Library of Congress, letter from J. D. to FDR, Mexico, September 4, 1939, (17). [Josephus Daniels was Secretary of the Navy in the cabinet of President Wilson from 1913 to 1921, and ambassador to Mexico, 1933-1942.]

14 Harold L. Ickes, *The Secret Diary of Harold L. Ickes,* Vol. II "The Inside Struggle, 1936-1939," New York: Simon and Schuster, 1954, p. 571. (Diary dated January 29, 1939)

15 *Ibid.,* p. 572.   16 *Ibid.,* p. 721.

17 Elliott Roosevelt (ed.), *op. cit.,* (1928-1945), Vol. 4, FDR to Harold Ickes (Memorandum in FDRL), The White House, September 16, 1939, p. 922. The editor reports that Ickes had been invited to address a large Polish meeting which Cordell Hull discouraged him from attending.

18 FDR, PPF 104, 1933-1945. To Marvin H. McIntyre from Cornelius Vanderbilt, September 27, 1933. A large file of correspondence and detailed reports from Vanderbilt to the President is available at Hyde Park. Many of these reports are addressed to the personal staff of the President such as Miss Margaret LeHand, secretary, and Colonel Edwin Martin Watson, personal aide, as well as Marvin H. McIntire, member of the secretariat. We may assume that the President saw a number of these reports through the years. One very pessimistic report on the state of public opinion dated October 24, 1939, had a note attached—"For the President," signed by Colonel Watson. It should be noted that Vanderbilt's reports were very frank expositions of public opinion as he encountered it on his lecture tours. Formal polling procedures were not involved.

19 FDR, PPF 104. Letter from Cornelius Vanderbilt, Jr. to the President, September 26, 1939.

20 *Ibid.,* October 5, 1939.   21 *Ibid.,* October 24, 1939.

22 Robert A. Divine, *The Illusion of Neutrality* (Chicago: The University of Chicago Press, 1962), p. 281. See pp. 281-85 for an excellent analysis of the failure to achieve revision of the Neutrality Act before the outbreak of the war. I have given only the barest outline of the conclusions presented in this study.

23 *Ibid.,* p. 284.

24 *The Radio Addresses of Col. Charles A. Lindbergh,* 1939-1940. (New York: Scribner's Commentator, 1940), pp. 1-7. Lindbergh delivered two important speeches during the fight against neutrality revision. They are so remarkable in their analysis that it is of interest to quote two short excerpts here.

On September 15, 1939, Lindbergh said: "America has little to gain in another European war. We must not be misguided by this foreign propaganda to the effect that our frontiers lie in Europe. One need only glance at a map to see where our true frontiers lie. What more could we ask than the Atlantic Ocean on the east and the Pacific on the west? No, our interests in Europe need not be from the standpoint of defense. Our own natural frontiers are enough for that. If we extend them to the center of Europe, we might as well extend them around the earth. An ocean is a formidable barrier, even for modern aircraft." (p. 3)

In an address entitled "Neutrality and War" delivered on October 13, 1939, the aviator declared: "I do not believe that repealing the arms embargo would assist democracy in Europe because I do not believe this is a war for democracy. This is a war over the balance of power in Europe—a war brought about by the desire for strength on the part of Germany and the fear of strength on the part of England and France. The more munitions the armies obtain, the longer the war goes on, and the more devastated Europe becomes, the less hope there is for democracy." (p. 6)

25 One of the most effective organizations fighting neutrality revision was the Citizens National "Keep America Out of War" Committee under the chairmanship of Hamilton Fish. In a subheading of their newsletter this organization referred to itself as "A Consolidation of Patriotic Organization Leaders and Citizens Representative of Every Phase of Our National Life, Banded together to Fight to Keep America Out of Foreign Wars." A newsletter issued to the public on September 2, 1939, said in part: "You can start at once to help prevent sabotage of the present neutrality laws which the War Makers will again attempt as soon as Congress is called in either Special or Regular Session. Help awaken others to this impending threat using and getting friends to use our KEEP U.S. OUT OF WAR letter-seals, autoplates and other neutrality materials, . . ." September 2, 1939, FDR, PPF 1561.

26 Divine, *op. cit.*, pp. 305-306.

CHAPTER IV

1 Elliott Roosevelt (ed.), *op. cit.*, (1928-1945) Vol. 4, p. 968.

2 Divine, *op. cit.*, p. 297.

3 Press Conference #636-A. At the previous annual conference for members of the American Society of Newspaper Editors, the President explained at some length the possible impact for the United States of a Nazi victory in Europe. (See Press Conference #540-A, April 20, 1939).

4 Langer and Gleason, *Challenge to Isolation*, pp. 429-435.

5 Press Conference #636-A, pp. 17-18.

6 Press Conference, #636-A, pp. 27-28.

7 Conference #645-A, May 23, 1940.

8 Rauch (ed.), *op. cit.*, p. 268. (Letter to Carl Sandburg, December 3, 1940.)

9 Conference #649-A. The 89-page transcript of this conference sheds an interesting light on the attitudes of a segment of American youth as well as those of the President when fielding some tough questions. Rauch (ed.), *op. cit.*, p. 237, said of this conference that "probably no President has submitted to a more severe raking over. . . ."

10 Rauch (ed.), *op. cit.*, p. 251.

11 A. L. Rowse provides a fascinating study of the British political environment during the 1930's. See his book *Appeasement: A Study in Political Decline 1933-1939* (New York: W. W. Norton & Co., 1961).

12 Key Pittman Papers, Subject File, 1910-1940, Foreign Affairs to Neutrality 1939, 150, Library of Congress.

CHAPTER V

1 Ickes, *op. cit.*, Vol. III, p. 191.

2 Langer and Gleason, *The Challenge to Isolation, op. cit.*, p. 471.

3 "What had particularly worried Bill [Douglas] was that Congressmen on the Hill have begun to express the conviction that the President, with respect to the international situation, might prove to be a Chamberlain. He feels as I do about the President's speech last Sunday night. As a matter of fact, everyone with whom I have talked has said that that speech was disappointing, except Ross McIntire [the President's physician], who, while not enthusiastic about it, thought it was adequate." Ickes, Vol. 3, *op. cit.*, p. 191.

4 Reference here is particularly to his messages to Congress (January 3 and May 16) and to his address at the University of Virginia (June 10) and before the Teamsters Union Convention (September 11). His May 16th message to Congress on national defense was certainly a frank call for increased vigilance and expenditures but as on other occasions the request is rationalized by emphasizing the need to bar the invasion of any part of the American hemisphere. Deliberate limitations of strategic analysis of the developments in Western Europe to the American hemisphere gave the American public only a limited insight into the full significance for the United States of military developments in Europe.

5 Elliott Roosevelt (ed.), *op. cit.*, (1928-1945) Vol. 4, FDR to Sayre, December 31, 1940, p. 1093.

6 *Ibid.*, pp. 1094-95.

7 Henry L. Stimson and McGeorge Bundy, *On Active Service in Peace and War* (New York: Harper & Brothers, 1947), p. 374.

8 Joseph C. Grew, *Ten Years in Japan* (New York: Simon and Schuster, 1944), p. 362. See also FDR, Official File 197, 1933-1945, O.F. 197-A Misc., Box 1.

9 *Ibid.*, p. 363.

10 Stimson, *op. cit.*, p. 366.

11 *Ibid.*

12 *Ibid.*, p. 368.

13 *Ibid.*, p. 369.

14 *Ibid.*, pp. 370-71. (Diary, April 25, 1941)

15 *Ibid.*, p. 375, 376.

16 FDR, PPF 1820, Group 13, 1941, Box 7, F 5/31/41, Letter from Henry L. Stimson to the President.

17 In connection with the Lend-Lease Bill an interesting telegram was found in the files requesting information on British financial sacrifices so that this information could be utilized in justifying the legislation to Americans. The

telegram, sent out over Harry Hopkins' signature, said in part: "You will understand that this attitude is not that of our Government but represents a lack of understanding on the part of the general public. Is it possible for you to arrange in some appropriate manner for a statement to be made in England at an early date indicating the great increase in your tax levies and any other financial sacrifices which the British people are making because of the war." FDR, PPF 4096, Harry Hopkins. Telegram from the White House, February 17, 1941, Harry Hopkins to Winston Churchill.

CHAPTER VI

1 FDR, PPF 91, Harvard University, 1933-1941. Telegram to the President from James Bryant Conant, June 5, 1940, and response.

2 FDR, PPF 1914, Letter from L. W. Douglas, June 5, 1940, to the President. President's reply to Douglas, June 7, 1940. Douglas had an academic, political, and business background. He was appointed ambassador to Great Britain in 1947.

3 FDR, PPF 91, Harvard University, 1933-1941. Letter from Conant to President Roosevelt, December 16, 1940. Reply December 19, 1940.

4 Public Papers, 1940, Vol. 9, op. cit., pp. 563-64.

5 Ibid., pp. 604-15. In this press conference the President makes his famous analogy between making supplies available to the British and lending a garden hose if the neighbor's house is on fire.

6 A memorandum prepared for Secretary of the Treasury Morgenthau which found its way into the President's speech file refers to several astute newspaper commentators who agree "that American uneasiness at present is due to a form of schizophrenia – a split of the national personality, one portion of which desires ardently to remain at peace, while the other portion insists upon a defeat of the Axis." The writer goes on to state that "public opinion polls now show plainly that this country has solved its problem on the intellectual level. It has been persuaded that the sensible thing for it to do is to aid the British – even at the risk of war. But the vital responses of a nation are not rational; they are emotional. And this nation has not yet been fired emotionally or stirred to the sacrifices which are demanded for heroic action." FDR, Group 13, PPF 1820, 1941, Box 7. Memorandum to Secretary Morgenthau from Alan Barth, May 16, 1941. Speech file May 31, 1941.

7 FDR, Group 13, PPF 1820, Box 7. Letter from Hamilton Fish Armstrong, May 6, 1941.

8 See excellent study by Trefousse which confirms these assumptions. H. L. Trefousse, Germany and American Neutrality, 1939-1941 (New York: Bookman Associates, 1951).

9 Letter from Hamilton Fish Armstrong, May 6, 1941, op. cit.

10 Ibid.

11 FDR, Group 13, PPF 1820, Box 7. Memorandum to the President, May 8, 1941, from Eugene Casey to the President. Review of a conversation between R. J. Finnegan, editor of the Chicago Daily Times with Bishop Sheil.

12 FDR, PPF 540, File of James P. Warburg, June 6, 1941.

13 Raymond H. Dawson, *The Decision to Aid Russia, 1941: Foreign Policy and Domestic Politics* (Chapel Hill: The University of North Carolina Press, 1959, p. 102. The author cites many quotations to illustrate this point.

14 FDR, PPF 1124, William C. Bullitt, 1933-1944. Letter from Bullitt to the President, July 1, 1941.

15 Ickes, Vol. III, *op. cit.*, pp. 549-550.

CHAPTER VII

1 Elliott Roosevelt (ed.), *op. cit.*, (1928-1945), Vol. 4, pp. 948-85. F.D.R. to Crown Prince Olav in Oslo, The White House, January 4, 1940.

2 William L. Langer and S. Everett Gleason, *The Undeclared War, 1940-1941* (New York: Harper & Brothers, 1953), p. 444.

3 FDR, PPF 1124, William Allen White, 1934-1944. Letter from F.D.R. to White, January 16, 1941.

4 Elliott Roosevelt (ed.), *op. cit.*, (1928-1954), Vol. 4, F.D.R. to Josiah W. Bailey in Washington, May 13, 1941, p. 1154.

5 Public Papers, 1941, Vol. 10, *op. cit.*, Press Conference #744, May 23, 1941, p. 177.

6 "As you know, I have to watch this Congress and public opinion like a hawk. . . ." Elliott Roosevelt (ed.) *op. cit.*, (1928-1945), Vol. 4, F.D.R. to Mackenzie King in Ottawa, September 27, 1941, p. 1216.

7 FDR, PPF 1820, Letter from Hadley Cantril to Mrs. Anna M. Rosenberg, March 20, 1941. Professor Cantril was connected with the Princeton Public Opinion Research Project. There is evidence that the President suggested questions for these polls. Additional material on this subect may be found in Professor Cantril's files at Princeton University. There is also evidence that the President submitted questions to the Gallup Poll through Mrs. Rosenberg and that she regularly forwarded these results of the Gallup and Princeton polls. A memorandum prepared for the President on October 18, 1941, tells of a telephone conversation in which Mrs. Rosenberg reports the answers to questions which had been previously submitted. The memorandum states that another question is being submitted to the poll "with the change suggested by the President." FDR, 1561, Box 3, Memorandum for the President, October 18, 1941. See an earlier memorandum from Edwin M. Watson to FDR, May 16, 1941, cited in Elliott Roosevelt (ed.), *op. cit.*, (1928-1945), Vol. 4, p. 1158.

8 FDR, PPF 1820, Group 13, 1941, Box 7, Filed 5/2/41. Telegram dated May 19, 1941, from Mrs. W. T. Dynn, Greenville, Mississippi. (Contained editorial). In connection with this speech also see public statement sent to the White House signed by Lewis W. Douglas and Mrs. J. Borden Harriman which closed with the statement ". . . we await the facts and leadership which our Commander-in-Chief alone can give." FDR, PPF 1820, Group 13, 1941, Box 7, Filed 5/31/41.

9 FDR, PPF 1820, Group 13, 1941, Box 7, Filed 5/31/41.

10 Wendell L. Willkie's remarkable leadership in vigorously supporting all-out aid to England after the 1940 Presidential elections has not been examined here. A fine presentation of his views ("I feel that perhaps the American people have

not yet fully grasped the extent of the crisis, or of their responsibility with regard to it." p. 870) may be found in Hearings before the Committee on Foreign Relations, U.S. Senate, Seventy-Seventh Congress, First Session on S. 275. A Bill Further to Promote the Defense of the United States, and for Other Purposes. Part 3, February 11, 1941, pp. 870-903. President Roosevelt appreciated Willkie's role in the fight against the hard-core isolationists. Roosevelt, in extending an invitation to Willkie to dedicate the Mount Rushmore memorial in South Dakota, added: "I would be ingenuous if I did not also mention that, geographically, this region is sadly in need of the kind of speeches you have been making." Elliott Roosevelt (ed.), op. cit., (1928-1945), Vol. 4, p. 1200.

11 Adler, The Isolationist Impulse, op. cit., p. 288.

12 Bernard Fensterwald, Jr., "The Anatomy of American 'Isolationism' and Expansionism," Part I, The Journal of Conflict Resolution, Vol. II, No. 1, (1958), p. 125.

CHAPTER VIII

1 Harry S. Truman, Mr. Citizen (New York: Bernard Geis Associates, 1953), p. 261.

2 Ibid., p. 262.

3 Ibid., p. 263. (President Truman expressed similar views in an interview with this writer, March 15, 1962, at the Truman Library.)

4 S. J. Woolf, "President Truman: A Portrait and Interview," The New York Times Magazine, October 14, 1945, p. 47. (Through the years the consistency of the President's statements on the relationship between leadership and public opinion is striking. The President's views must have been well formulated at the time he took his oath of office, for the views expressed in this interview on October 14, 1945, are identical to views expressed in an interview that he granted this writer seventeen years later in Independence, Missouri.)

5 Remarks of the President to the "Flying Classroom" American Association of School Administrators in the Rose Garden, July 9, 1948, Truman Library. (Hereafter cited as TL)

6 Clinton L. Rossiter, "The American President," Yale Review, Vol. XXXVII, No. 4 (June, 1948), p. 628.

7 Harry S. Truman, Memoirs, Vol. 2, (Garden City, New York: Doubleday, 1955), p. 177. The President no doubt would agree with the following maxim by Jefferson: "If we think them [the people] not enlightened enough to exercise their control with a wholesome discretion, the remedy is not to take it from them, but to inform their discretion by education." James Reston, "The Scientific Revolution and Democracy," New York Times, March 7, 1962, p. 32.

8 Truman, Mr. Citizen, op. cit., p. 264.

9 Seymour H. Fersh, The View from the White House (Washington: Public Affairs Press, 1961), p. 111.

10 Address of the President delivered at the Imperial Council Session of the Shrine of North America, at Soldier Field, Chicago, July 19, 1949. TL

11 OR 1, Columbia, Missouri, Address delivered at the commencement exercises at the University of Missouri, June 9, 1950. TL

12 We have noted the close similarity of views between Presidents Truman

and Wilson on this subject. Wilson also wrote that the President is the "spokesman for the real sentiment and purpose of the country, by giving direction to opinion, by giving the country at once the information and the statements of policy which will enable it to form its own judgments alike of parties and of men. . . ." Moreover, the President's is "the only national voice in affairs. Let him once win the admiration and confidence of the country, and no other single force can withstand him, no combination of forces will easily overpower him. His position takes the imagination of the country. He is representative of no constituency, but of the whole people." Woodrow Wilson, *Constitutional Government in the United States,* (New York: Columbia University Press, 1911), p. 68.

13 Truman, *Mr. Citizen, op. cit.,* p. 264.

14 Walter Lippmann's views of President Roosevelt's press conferences were very critical: "Roosevelt's conduct of press conferences became, as time went on, more a form of personal recreation than a means of public education. As he got his exercise in the swimming pool, so he exercised his wits in his press conferences. Less and less came out of them which gave substance to the freedom of the press. More and more they degenerated into persiflage by means of which the President, who was nearly always the victor, would win for himself a few more days of freedom from the inquisitiveness of the press." "Mr. Truman's Press Conference," *Washington Post,* October 11, 1946.

15 Elmer E. Cornwell, Jr. "The Presidential Press Conference: A Study in Institutionalization," *Midwest Journal of Political Science,* Vol. IV, No. 4 (November, 1960), p. 378.

16 Bert Andrews, "Truman Holds His Hundredth Press Parley," *New York Herald Tribune,* March 27, 1947.

17 Press and Radio Conference #103, Executive Office of the President, April 17, 1947.

18 Remarks made after signing the Greek-Turkish Bill, Kansas City, Mo., May 22, 1947. TL

19 "Informal Remarks of the President To A Group of Guests Of The National Association of Broadcasters," Executive Office of the President, June 26, 1947. TL

20 Remarks of the President to a Group from the National Association of Radio News Editors, Executive Office of the President, November 13, 1947. TL A record of these remarks may be found in OR 1 at the Truman Library. Only the first item was included in the *Public Papers of the Presidents — Harry S. Truman—1947.* See Remarks of the President, April 27, where he also stresses the importance of the news media. Interesting information regarding the President's newspaper reading habits may be found in the record of the National Conference of Editorial Writers, Executive Office, October 17, 1947. See *Public Papers,* 1947, pp. 470-471. The President stated that his newspapers were not screened and that he read at least a dozen papers every day. He also indicated that he looked at editorials that were sent to him from out of town. Among the papers he listed were the Washington and New York dailies, *Baltimore Sun* and *Philadelphia Bulletin.* He also mentioned the *St. Louis Post-Dispatch* and an occasional examination of the Pittsburgh papers, *Kansas City Star, Chicago Sun.* There is no doubt that this wide listing of papers should have given the press corps satisfaction.

CHAPTER IX

1 W. W. Rostow, *The United States in the World Arena: An Essay in Recent History*, op. cit., p. 143.

2 *Ibid.*, p. 185.

3 *Ibid.* Quoted from Arthur Bliss Lane, *I Saw Poland Betrayed* (New York: Bobbs-Merrill, 1948), p. 195.

4 Edmund Stillman and William Pfaff, *The New Politics: America and the End of the Post-War World* (New York: Coward McCann, 1961), p. 19.

5 Secretary of State Byrnes left the State Department on January 20, 1947.

6 Rostow, op. cit., p. 178-180.

7 Jerome S. Bruner, *Mandate From The People* (New York: Duell, Sloan and Pearce, 1944), p. 106. See also Warren B. Walsh, "What the American People Think of Russia," *The Public Opinion Quarterly*, Vol. 8, No. 4, 1944, pp. 513-22.

8 Nancy Boardman Eddy, *Public Opinion and United States Foreign Policy, 1937-1956*, American Project, Working Paper, MIT, n.d., p. 40.

9 *The Conference of Berlin* (The Potsdam Conference), 1945. Two volumes. Department of State Publications 7015 and 7163. Washington, D. C.: Government Printing Office, 1960. See particularly, Vol. 1, pp. 24-81.

10 Thomas A. Bailey, *A Diplomatic History of the American People*, Sixth Ed. (New York: Appleton-Century-Crofts, Inc., 1958), p. 777.

11 Frank Freidel, *America in the Twentieth Century* (New York: Alfred A. Knopf, 1960), p. 467.

12 John M. Fenton, *In Your Opinion* . . . (Boston: Little Brown and Company, 1960), pp. 82-83.

CHAPTER X

1 Bailey, op. cit., p. 778.

2 Freidel, op. cit., p. 473.

3 Forrestal has been referred to as a tower of strength not only because of his stand against demobilization and his fight for compulsory military service but also because of his constant urging that the remaining military forces be utilized strategically. See William Henry Chamberlin, *Beyond Containment* (Chicago: Henry Regnery Company, 1953), p. 54.

4 Rostow, op. cit., p. 179.

5 *Ibid.*, p. 267. See study by Nancy Boardman Eddy, *Public Opinion and United States Foreign Policy, 1937-1956*, op. cit.

6 Walter Millis (ed.), *The Forrestal Diaries* (New York: The Viking Press, 1951), p. 9.

7 *Ibid.*, p. 93. Also see pp. 214-15 for quotations from letters written by Forrestal on this subject.

8 *Ibid.*, p. 102.

9 OF 190-R, Demobilization. [see particularly 0-818, Folder # 1 for this story. TL]

10 Interview with President Truman, op. cit.

11 Press and Radio Conference #144, Executive Office of the President, April 23, 1948, p. 5, TL.

12 OF 190-R, 0-818, (December 1945), Demobilization File. Earl G. Harrison was vice chairman of the FPA. TL.

13 OF 190-R (January 1946), Folder #1 (0-818), TL.

14 *Ibid.*

15 *Ibid.* In regard to the question of our military strength in the post-war world some credit must go to F.D.R. In mentioning UMT in his State of the Union Message on January 6, 1945, he demonstrated foresight and political courage. He said: "I am clear in my own mind that, as an essential factor in the maintenance of world peace in the future, we must have universal military training after this war, and I shall send a special message to the Congress on this subject." F.D.R., Public Papers, 1944-1945, Vol. 13, *op.cit.*, 126-A Radio Address, January 6, 1945, p. 515.

CHAPTER XI

1 Truman, *Memoirs*, Vol. 1, *op. cit.*, pp. 411-412.

2 Press and Radio Conference #179, April 22, 1949.

3 Harry S. Truman, *Truman Speaks* (New York: Columbia University, 1960), p. 71.

4 Truman, *Memoirs*, Vol. 1, *op. cit.*, p. 15 (Report from the State Department to the President, April 13, 1945).

5 Off the record remarks of the President to the American Society of Newspaper Editors, Washington, D. C., April 17, 1948, p. 3-4. TL.

6 *Ibid.*, p. 6.   7 *Forrestal Diaries, op. cit.*, p 50.   8 *Ibid.*

9 Truman, *Truman Speaks*, p. 10.

10 Address of the President, Army Day in Chicago, April 6, 1946.

11 *Public Papers*, Harry S. Truman, 1947. Address on foreign economic policy, Baylor University, March 6, 1947, p. 167.

12 Address delivered by the President at the site of the Jefferson National Expansion Memorial, St. Louis, June 10, 1950.

CHAPTER XII

1 Fenton, *op. cit.*, p. 75.   2 *Ibid.*, p. 76.

3 *New York Times*, February 11, 1946, p. 28.

4 *Congressional Record*, Vol. 92, Part 2, 79th Congress, 2nd Session, February 27, 1946, pp. 1692-1695. (Senator Vandenberg served as an American delegate in the first General Assembly.)

5 Andrei Y. Vyshinsky represented the Soviet Union on the Security Council; he was first deputy minister for Foreign Affairs.

6 *New York Times*, March 1, 1946, p. 10.

7 John F. Dulles was one of President Truman's consultants on foreign affairs.

8 *Congressional Record*, Senate, March 12, 1946, *op. cit.*, p. 2139.

9 *New York Times*, March 13, 1946.

10 Department of State, *Report on American Opinion*, March 6, 1946. (Hereafter cited as *Report on American Opinion* with date.)

11 *Report on American Opinion*, March 21, 1946.

12 Winston Churchill, "Alliance of English-Speaking People," *Vital Speeches,* Vol. XII, No. 11 (March 15, 1946), pp. 329-32. [see also Frank Freidel, *America in the Twentieth Century, op. cit.,* p. 468.]

13 One writer has commented that Churchill broached no new ideas at Fulton; however, now "for the first time they were given wide reportorial coverage." William Frank Zarnow, *America at Mid-Century* (Cleveland, Ohio: Howard Allen, Inc., 1959), pp. 18-19.

14 *Report on American Opinion,* March 18, 1946.

15 Freidel, *op. cit.,* p. 467   16 Goldman, *op. cit.,* p. 38.

17 *New York Times,* March 9, 1946, p. 12.

18 Herbert Agar, *The Price of Power: America Since 1945* (Chicago: The University of Chicago Press, 1957), p. 59.

19 Freidel, *op. cit.,* p. 468.   20 Goldman, *op. cit.,* p. 38.

21 Jonathan Daniels, *The Man of Independence* (Philadelphia: Lippincott, 1950), p. 312. [See another account by Alfred Steinberg, *The Man From Missouri* (New York: G. P. Putnam's Sons, 1962), pp. 279-81.]

22 *New York Times,* March 7, 1946, p. 1.

23 *Report on American Opinion,* November 5, 1946.

24 *Ibid.,* October 1947.

25 Survey Research Center, University of Michigan, April 1947. *Public Attitudes Toward Russia and United States Relations — A Nation-wide Survey,* Part II, p 34, Table 32.

26 *Ibid.,* Part I, p. 8. "Getting tough" with the Russians was a popular phrase used at this time to describe one particular approach toward the Soviet Union. [See this study for an indication of the variety of meanings attached to this popular term. To half of the group questioned this phrase meant "not giving in" or not "backing down."]

27 *Report on American Opinion,* June 1947.   28 *Ibid.,* September 1947.

29. *Ibid.,* July 1949. [An indication of the temper of public opinion is demonstrated by a survey which indicates that 81 per cent of a national cross section continued to favor the maintenance of American occupation in Germany. February 1949.]

30 *Report on American Opinion,* March 1950.   31 NORC, August 1950.

32 *Report on American Opinion,* February 1951.

CHAPTER XIII

1 Hans J. Morgenthau, *The Purpose of American Politics, op cit.,* p. 132.

2 Robert E. Elder, "The Public Studies Division of the Department of State: Public Opinion Analysts in the Formulation and Conduct of American Foreign Policy," *The Western Political Quarterly,* Vol. X, No. 4 (December 1957), p. 783.

3 Barbara Ward, *The West at Bay* (New York: W. W. Norton & Company, 1948), p. 112.

4 Louis J. Halle, *Dream and Reality: Aspects of American Foreign Policy,* p. 296.

5 James Reston, "Bewildered Congress Faces World Leadership Decision," *New York Times,* March 1947.

6 Marshall succeeded James F. Byrnes as Secretary of State in January 1947.

7 J. M. Jones, Box 1, Drafts of the Truman Doctrine, Memorandum for the

File, March 12, 1947. TL. [This Memorandum is partly based on hearsay from Acheson and others concerned.]

8 *Ibid.*

9 Eric F. Goldman reports that when Senator Vandenberg left the White House on February 27, 1947, he is supposed to have remarked to President Truman: "Mr. President, if that's what you want, there's only one way to get it. That is to make a personal appearance before Congress and scare hell out of the country." Eric F. Goldman, *The Crucial Decade, America, 1954-1955* (New York: Alfred A. Knopf, 1956).

10 J. M. Jones, Box 1, Truman Doctrine "Important Relevant Papers," TL.

11 *Ibid.*

12 J. M. Jones, Box 1, Information and Program on United States Aid to Greece, TL.

13 *Forrestal Diaries, op. cit.*, p. 251, 252.

14 Norman A. Graebner (ed.), *An Uncertain Tradition: American Secretaries of State in the Twentieth Century, op. cit.*, p. 254.

15 Walter Lippmann, "On Borrowed Time," *Washington Post*, May 10, 1947.

16 Harry Bayard Price, *The Marshall Plan and Its Meaning* (Ithaca, New York: Cornell University Press, 1955). See Chapter 2—"Emergence of the Marshall Plan", particularly pp. 41-46.

17 Arthur H. Vandenberg, *The Private Papers of Senator Vandenberg* (ed. by Arthur H. Vandenberg, Jr. with the collaboration of Joe Max Morris) (Boston: Houghton Mifflin, 1952), p. 375.

18 *Ibid.*, p. 380.　　　　　　　　　　19 *Ibid.*, p. 381.

20 Joseph and Stewart Alsop, "The Home Front," *Washington Post*, July 9, 1947.

21 Henry L. Stimson, "The Challenge to Americans," *Foreign Affairs*, Vol. 26 (October, 1947), p. 14. (The views expressed here are very similar to those held by President Truman.)

22 Committee for the Marshall Plan, Executive Committee — Minutes and Agenda—1947. First recorded Memorandum: October 30, 1947. A Statement of Purpose: The Committee for the Marshall Plan to Aid European Recovery, p. 4, TL.

23 Minutes of the Executive Committee Meeting, Committee for the Marshall Plan, Biltmore Hotel, New York City, January 23, 1948. TL. [Judge Robert P. Patterson, Presiding Chairman. One of the Committee members raised the question of whether the estimated $25,000 required to print the booklet could not be more effectively utilized by paying for eight or ten radio broadcasts.]

24 With respect to this time lapse Secretary of State Marshall notes that procedures involved have been characteristic of the democratic process. He commented: "All of this procedure is as we would have it. It is but an expression of a democracy of free men carefully considering and debating what had best be done." There is, however, the consideration that with this kind of delay the "initial advantage" rests with the authoritarian government. While expressing confidence that "democracies will invariably win out," he is troubled by the thought "that the lapse of time may result in such a serious loss of position and strength that the task of the democracies may involve a long, hard struggle to recover the ground thus lost." George C. Marshall, "Our Dominant Position of Leadership: Timely Action Required," delivered at the University of California,

Berkeley, California, March 19, 1948. *Vital Speeches*, Vol. 14 (April 1, 1948), pp. 358-59.

25 *Forrestal Diaries, op. cit.,* p. 397.

26 *Vital Speeches, op cit.,* pp. 355-56. (President Truman, blaming Russia for violating the Yalta and Potsdam agreements and sabotaging all efforts to establish peace, reiterated these three recommendations in another speech on the same day before the Society of the Friendly Sons of St. Patrick in New York. See John C. Campbell, *The United States in World Affairs, 1947-1948* (New York: Harper & Brothers, 1948), p. 507.

27 *Forrestal Diaries, op. cit.,* p. 384.

28 W. W. Rostow, *The United States in the World Arena: An Essay in Recent History, op. cit.,* p. 235.

29 Glenn D. Paige, *The Korean Decision*, Department of Political Science, Northwestern University, Evanston, Illinois, July 1, 1959, p. 135.

30 Richard C. Snyder, et al. (ed.), *Foreign Policy Decision Making: An Approach to the Study of International Politics* (New York: The Free Press of Glencoe, 1962), p. 209. [See "U.S. Decision to Resist Aggression in Korea" by Richard C. Snyder and Glenn D. Paige.]

31 Truman, *Mr. Citizen, op. cit.,* p. 262.

CHAPTER XIV

1 H. Schuyler Foster, "American Public Opinion and U.S. Foreign Policy," *The Department of State Bulletin*, Vol. XLI, No. 1066 (November 30, 1959), p. 797, citing Christian A. Herter.

2 *Ibid.,* p. 803.

3 W. Phillips Davison, *The Berlin Blockade: A Study in Cold War Politics* (Princeton, New Jersey: Princeton University Press, 1958), p. 381.

4 E. Malcolm Carroll, *Germany and the Great Powers, 1899-1914: A Study in Public Opinion and Foreign Policy* (New York: Prentice-Hall, Inc., 1938), p. viii.

5 William S. White, *Majesty and Mischief: A Mixed Tribute to F.D.R.* (New York: McGraw Hill Book Co., Inc., 1961), p. 60.

6 Dexter Perkins, 'The American Attitude Towards War," *The Yale Review*, Vol. XXXVIII, No. 2 (December, 1948), p. 249.

7 Sumner Welles, *Where Are We Heading?* (New York: Harper & Brothers, 1946), p. 19.

8 John W. Masland, "Pressure Groups and American Foreign Policy," *The Public Opinion Quarterly*, Vol. 6 (Spring, 1942), p. 122.

9 Elmer Davis, "Vox Populi and Foreign Policy," *Harper's Magazine*, Vol. 204 (June, 1952), p. 70.

10 See more detailed discussion of this point in Roger Hilsman, "Congressional-Executive Relations and the Foreign Policy Consensus," *The American Political Science Review*, Vol. LII, No. 3 (September, 1958), p. 741.

11 Arthur Schlesinger, Jr., *The Public Opinion Quarterly*, Vol. 15, No. 1, *op. cit.,* p. 149.

12 Louis J. Halle, *Dreams and Reality: Aspects of American Foreign Policy, op. cit.,* p. 304.

13 James N. Rosenau, "Consensus, Leadership and Foreign Policy," *SAIS Review*, Vol. 6, No. 2 (Winter, 1962), p. 4.

14 Murray Edelman, *The Symbolic Uses of Politics* (Urbana: University of Illinois Press, 1964), p. 76.

15 *Ibid.*, p. 172.

16 Dean Rusk, "A Fresh Look at the Formulation of Foreign Policy," *U.S. Department of State Bulletin*, Vol. 44 (March, 1961), p. 398.

17 William H. Nelson (ed.), *Theory and Practice in American Politics* (Chicago: University of Chicago Press, 1964), p. 122.

18 Carl J. Friedrich has said that the belief in the common man is based on three vital assumptions: "First, ordinary men, when confronted with a problem, finding themselves in a 'jam,' will think hard and get all the facts they can. Second, they will reach sensible conclusions as to the right way to get out of the jam—right technically and morally. Common men will reach such conclusions without the help of 'experts,' and it is part of their 'common sense' to recognize an expert when they see one. That is what the belief in the common man implies as to the mind. But it is equally important that, third, the common man is believed to possess the character to go through with the solution, to follow the right road as seen, to act rationally as well as to think rationally." Carl J. Friedrich, *The New Image of The Common Man* (Boston: The Beacon Press, 1950), pp. 5-6.

19 Edelman, *The Symbolic Uses of Politics*, p. 91.

20 Formosa, 1955; Middle East, 1957; Cuba, 1962.

21 Senator Aiken's comments probably reflected the hesitant acquiescence of other thoughtful citizens: "It has been apparent to me for some months that the expansion of the war in Southeast Asia was inevitable. I felt that it shouldn't occur, but the decision wasn't mine. I am still apprehensive of the outcome of the President's decision, but he felt that the interest of the United States required prompt action. As a citizen I feel I must support our President whether his decision is right or wrong. I hope the present action will prove to be correct. I support the resolution with misgivings." *New York Times*, August 18, 1964, p. 18.

22 Dean Acheson, "The Responsibility for Decision in Foreign Policy," *The Yale Review*, Vol. XLIV, No. 1 (September 1954), p. 1.

INDEX

Acheson, Dean, 95, 112
Adler, Selig, 11, 62
Aid to Britain movement, 58-59
Almond, Gabriel, 4, 7
American Youth Conference, 33-35
apathy, role of, 7
Armstrong, Hamilton Fish, 11, 51-52
Axis powers, 41

Bailey, Thomas A., 71, 73
Beard, Charles A., 13
Berelson, Bernard, 5-6
Berle, Adolf A., 25
bipartisanship, 104-105
blockade, of Germany, 12
Bohlen, Charles E., 78-79
Borah, William E., 28
Bryce, James, 7
Bullitt, William C., 25, 40, 55-56
Bundy, McGeorge, 45-47
Byrnes, James F., 83-84

Cantril, Hadley, 18, 59
Carroll, E. Malcolm, 102
Chicago Daily News, editorials, 37-39
Churchill, Sir Winston S., "Iron Curtain" speech, 85-88; 112-113
Committee to Defend America by Aiding the Allies, 58
Conant, James Bryant, 49-51
Connally, Tom, 84
convoys, 45-46, 47
Coughlin, Father Charles E., 13, 27

Dahl, Robert A., 2
Daniels, Jonathan, 87-88
Daniels, Josephus, 25
Davis, Norman H., 14, 15
Dawson, Raymond H., 55
demobilization, 73-76
Divine, Robert A., 30-31
Douglas, Lewis W., 39, 40, 49
Draft Extension Act, 1941, 48
Drummond, Donald F., 19-20

Eagleton, Clyde, 23
Eden, Anthony, 14-15
Eichelberger, Clark, 29, 96-97
elections, role of, 2-3

Fenton, John 72, 81
Forrestal, James V., 73-74, 95, 99
"Fortress America" concept, 21, 66
Frankfurter, Felix, 53
Freidel, Frank, 71-72, 87
Fulbright, J. William, 10

Gerard, James W., 36
Germany, blockade of, 12
Gleason, S. Everett, 13, 19, 62
Greece, aid to, 68, 93-95, 104
Greenland, status of, 32-33
Grew, Joseph C., letter from Roosevelt, 44-45
Gulf of Tonkin Congressional Resolution, 111-112

Halle, Louis J., 92
Harriman Committee, 96
Herter, Christian A., 102
Hoover, Herbert, 29
House, Colonel Edward M., 11-12, 18
Hull, Cordell, 14, 15

Ickes, Harold, 26-27, 38, 39-40, 53, 54, 56
isolationism, Roosevelt reaction, 11; comment on, 13, 29, isolationist lobby, 15; in Congress, 19; Truman's view, 80

Jones, Joseph M., 93

Kennan, George W., 5
Key, V. O., 3, 8-9
Knox, Frank, 29, 37-39
Korean war, 99-101

Landon, Alfred M., 29

Langer, William L., 13, 19, 62
Lasswell, Harold, 9, 109
Lend-Lease Act, 45, 55, 56; planning for, 51
Lindbergh, Charles A., 29
Lindsay, A. D., 6
Lippmann, Walter, 5, 9, 95-96
Locarno Pacts, 12
Long, Huey, 13

MacLeish, Archibald, 39, 40
Marshall Plan, 95-98
May, Ernest R., 110
Mill, James, 10
Molotov, 78
Moore, R. Walton, 25
Morgenthau, Hans J., 2, 9
Munich agreement, 21, 70; crisis, 19-20

Neutrality Act, of 1935; 11, 13; of 1937, 14; of 1939, neutrality revision fight, 28-29
Nisbet, Robert A., 7

opinion elite, 4, 8, 106
opinion-makers, 4-5
Osgood, Robert E., 24-25

Paige, Glenn D., 100
Pearson, Lester, 8
Pegler, Westbrook, 17
Perkins, Dexter, 2, 105
postwar crises, 111-112
Potsdam Conference, 77-78
press conferences, comparison between Roosevelt and Truman, 67-68

Rauch, Basil, 13, 20, 23
Reston, James, 96
Rhineland, occupation of, 12
Roosevelt, Eleanor, 31-32, 33-34
Roosevelt, Franklin Delano, Chautauqua address, 13, 15; Quarantine Address, 15-18, 21, 106; Annual Message to Congress, 1939, 20;

"frontier on the Rhine" remarks, 22; fireside chat on European war, 31; "arsenal of democracy" speech, 41-42; campaign speeches, 1940, 42-43; annual message, 34-35
Rosenau, James N., 4, 109
Rosenberg, Anna M., 59
Rosenman, Samuel, 75-76
Rossiter, Clinton, 64-65
Rostow, Walt, 8, 69, 71
Rowse, A. L., 9-10
Rusk, Dean, 109-110

Sandburg, Carl, 33
Sayre, Francis B., 43-44
Schlesinger, Arthur, Jr., 8, 13
Sheil, Bishop Bernard, J., 52-53
Shils, Edward A., 7-8
Soviet Union, attacked by Germany, 54; American aid to, 55-56; U.S. relations with, 69-70; U.S. public sentiment for, 71-72; deterioration of public confidence in, 72, 108; Truman's view of, 77-78
Stalin, Iosif, speech of February 9, 1946, 81-82
Stimson, Henry L., 37, 39, 45-48, 97-98
Swing, Raymond Gram, 59-61

The American Voter, 3
Truman Doctrine, 92-95

Vandenberg, Senator Arthur H., 83, 96-97, 104
Vanderbilt, Cornelius, 27

Warburg, James, 53-54
Washington Post, 24, 97
Welles, Sumner, 14, 105
White, William Allen, 29, 30, 38-39, 58, 105
White, William S., 104
Wilson, Woodrow, 64, 67
Woodring, Harry H., 39
Wright, Quincy, 6